The Wool Clipper
GLENTANNER
New Zealand Immigration Ship 1857–1861

By Belinda Lansley

*Ancestral Journeys
of New Zealand
Series*

This book would not have been possible without the help of the following people. Special thanks to:

Jo Featherson, Forbes/Paterson information
Relda Smith, Information on William Forbes
The Turnbull Clan Association, Pringle and Hymers families
Stuart Lansley, for editing my work
and Marolyn Diver of Dornie Publishing.

Dornie Publishing Company

Grasmere, Invercargill
www.dorniepublishing.tk

Original text © Belinda Lansley 2013
Images © named individuals, institutions
All rights reserved
ISBN 978-0-473-23751-6

Cover Design by Strawberrymouse Designs

Dedicated to James Potts, *Glentanner* passenger

Belinda Lansley

Contents

Introduction	7
The Ship	9
First Voyage to New Zealand 1857	31
Passengers on the 1857 Voyage	55
Second Voyage to New Zealand 1861	79
Passengers on the 1861 Voyage	85
Passenger Lists	87
References	*98*

Introduction

This book covers the history of one of the lesser known ships that ferried migrants from Great Britain to New Zealand, the *Glentanner*.

I decided to write about the *Glentanner* as I had researched a man who was on board in 1857. His name was James Potts. He brought his future wife Sarah Winfield Brown out to New Zealand three years after he arrived here. They had a life of trials and I'm sure happiness as well, but then James died young, leaving Sarah a childless widow. Sarah remarried and was one of the most wonderful stepmothers to my great great grandmother and her sisters. Without James Potts' adventurous nature, Sarah would never have come to this side of the world to be a much admired stepmother.

All sources are referenced carefully at the back of this book. Some sources may have errors. Often in the past people exaggerated or made incorrect entries in the records. Advertisements for ships often made a ship sound better than it really was in order to gain passengers, just as advertisements operate these days. So I have worked with what was available and hope this written record is as accurate as possible.

There were not many accounts from this ship. If anyone has further information on the ship *Glentanner* including ship diaries, family letters or comments in their family histories about the journey that you are willing to share, please contact me so it can be added to any future updated editions.

Belinda Lansley

belinda.lansley@yahoo.co.nz

The Ship

The Wool Clipper *Glentanner*

The *Glentanner* was built in 1842 in Aberdeen, Scotland by Alexander Hall and Co., who were shipbuilders from 1790 to 1958. In 1839, they developed the Aberdeen or clipper bow, which improved speed and sailing performance. Alexander Hall died in 1849. His two sons, James and William, took over the business and built many famous clipper ships including the warship *Jho Sho Maru*. This ship nearly caught on fire due to a fire breaking out close by. The ship was moved to the middle of the dock away from the flames. James Hall died of a heart attack while fighting the blaze. His heart attack was thought to have been brought on by anxiety that his beloved warship could have been burned. The company also produced steamers and trawlers, coasters, tugs and dredgers. The company did not modernise after WWII and Hall Russell took over the company in 1957.[1]

The English-built emigrant ship Artemisia, which was built in 1847 and had a tonnage of 492 tons, not far off the statistics of the Glentanner. (The Illustrated London News, 12 August 1848.) No picture has been found as yet for the Glentanner.

The *Glentanner* was built from oak, fir and elm. In 1842, the ship was coppered and was partly fastened with iron bolts. It had three masts, a deck and one poop deck. There was also a male figurehead on the ship. It had a weight of 610 tons with a burden of about 1000 tons.[2] The weight of burden was a good guide as to the maximum cargo allowed on board that would make the journey economic, as well as making sure the weight was not exceeded, which could cause the ship to sink while at sea.[3]

The *Glentanner* was a clipper ship. The name "clipper ship" was a synonym for a merchant ship. They were first created by American ship builders in the 1840s and were extra fast, travelling on average 250 miles per day while other types of ships averaged 150 miles per day. English ship builders started to build them as well. They revolutionised sea transport and were wonderful ships to behold. Clipper ships had three masts and square sails, and it was this combination that made them so fast and popular in the 19th century.[3]

Glentanar or *Glentanner*

It appears that when the *Glentanner* was built it was named *Glentanar*[4] but was listed as *Glentanner* in Lloyd's Register of Ships.[2] Where the name *Glentanner* came from is not really known, although being built in Aberdeen it could be named after Glentanner Burn which is approximately 150 miles south of Aberdeen. There is also an estate named Glen Tanar which was opened in 1869 well after the *Glentanner* was built but is only 35 miles from Aberdeen.[5] It was likely a name in the area of Aberdeen. Documentation would be needed to prove where the ship's name originally came from.

Owners of the *Glentanner*

The first owner of the *Glentanner* was Yule & Co. of Liverpool, where the ship was first registered. The registration then moved to Aberdeen where it was owned by many owners who had part share in the ship. The last recorded owner of the ship was Hyde, Hodge & Co. who bought the ship in 1849 and the registration moved to London. The *Glentanner* slipped off Lloyd's Register of Ships in 1852 and doesn't appear again.[4] We do know that Vaughan & Co. bought the ship in 1858 from Hyde, Hodge & Co.[6] Also in 1861, when the ship came back to Lyttelton, the *Glentanner* had different owners again; Messrs. Wilson of Plymouth, England.[7]

Willis, Gann & Co.

Willis, Gann & Co. ran a line of packet ships from Great Britain to New Zealand in the early years of colonisation. A packet ship was originally used for shipping post office mail to the colonies and other places around the world, but this meaning was eventually extended to include passengers as well as mail.[8] Willis, Gann & Co. advertised regularly in English newspapers. The company was run by Arthur Willis, who, in 1839, was a Founding Director of the New Zealand Company which promoted the colonisation of New Zealand.[9] He was also a representative of Lloyds and a member of the London Society of Shipowners. He encouraged famous people such as Dr Julius Haast to travel to New Zealand and explore the land.[10]

In 1854, the provincial governments became responsible for immigration. The Province of Canterbury had the largest immigration scheme of all the provinces, bringing in almost a fifth of all immigrants between 1858 and 1870. Two thirds of all passengers arriving in Canterbury were assisted; generally, half of their fare was paid by the Provincial Government.[11]

Willis, Gann & Co. charged £8 in 1855–57 for a single farm labourer in steerage aboard the Clontarf.[12] The cost for the *Sebastopol* in 1861 was £13 10s, and reduced to exactly £13 by 1863. In 1863, rival company Messrs. Shaw, Savill & co. secured the contract for carrying emigrants to Otago, the fares being £12 from Glasgow and £13 10s from London.[13] In 1857, the rates for steerage passengers on the *Glentanner* were much more expensive, as follows:

Single man or woman	£20 10s
Couple	£41
Child	£10 5s
Infant	free

Second cabin passengers paid a bit more to have a cabin to themselves with rates as follows:

Single man or woman	£26
Couple	£52
Child	£13

In the *Glentanner* passenger lists there is no mention of the cost for chief cabin passengers. However for the *Clontarf* from 1855–57, Willis Gann & Co. were charging £60 for one person in a chief cabin measuring 6 by 7ft, or £40 per person for two people sharing a cabin. The second cabins were 6ft 9in by 7ft 6 in and for four people this cost £25 per person. Also available were second cabins for married couples measuring 3ft 6in by 7ft 8in at £25 per person.[12] It is likely Willis, Gann & Co. would have charged similar prices for the *Glentanner*.

The average annual wage for a housemaid in the 1850s–1860s was £11–£14.[14] Therefore, the full cost of the journey was a full year's wage. The average annual wage for a farm labourer in England and Wales in 1860 was £30 2s 4p[15], so the full cost of the journey was over a third of their annual wage. We can now see that travel to New Zealand was expensive and what a struggle it was to raise even half the fare. They often had help from family and friends already in the colony and, of course, the Provincial Government assisted by paying part of the fare.

Life on Board a Clipper Ship

The Willis, Gann & Co. chart from the 1855–1857 period, on the following page shows the food allocated to the different classes of passengers.[12] The second cabin and steerage passengers were the only ones who received lime juice to keep away the scurvy. Maybe the first class passengers received enough vitamin C from the extra muscatel raisins that were served to them. Records show that sometimes fowl were kept in coups for fresh eggs, and sometimes larger animals were kept on board for fresh meat. Water was stored in barrels but became stale and often grew algae or had vermin fall in and die. Food was stored in lidded barrels, but if someone left the lid off they could often become contaminated with rat and mice droppings. The bad hygiene often led to dysentery, cholera and many deaths on board. Flour often had weevils.

Weekly Dietary Scale for each Adult Passenger.

Articles.	Chief Cabin.	Second Cabin.	Steerage.
Preserved Meats	1½ lb.	1½ lb.	1 lb.
Preserved Salmon	½ ”	—	—
Assorted Soups	1 ”	—	—
Soup and Bouilli	—	½ lb.	—
York Ham	1 ”	½ ”	—
Tripe	½ ”	—	—
Fish	½ ”	¼ lb.	—
Prime India Beef	½ ”	1 ”	1¼ lb.
Irish Mess Pork	1 ”	1½ ”	1 ”
Biscuit	3 ”	4¼ ”	3½ ”
Flour	4¼ ”	4¼ ”	3 ”
Rice	1 ”	1 ”	½ ”
Barley	¼ ”	½ ”	—
Peas	½ pint	½ pint	½ pint
Oatmeal	½ ”	½ ”	1 ”
Preserved Milk	½ ”	—	—
Sugar, refined	¾ lb.	—	—
Sugar, raw	¾ ”	1 lb.	1 lb.
Lime Juice	—	6 oz.	6 oz.
Tea	3 oz.	1½ oz.	1½ oz.
Coffee	5 ”	3 ”	2 ”
Butter	½ lb.	½ lb.	6 ”
Cheese	½ ”	¼ ”	—
Currants	¼ ”	¼ ”	—
Raisins, Valentia	½ ”	½ ”	½ lb.
Raisins, Muscatel	¼ ”	—	—
Suet	½ ”	6 oz.	6 oz.
Preserved Carrots	½ ”	—	—
Pickles	¼ pint	¼ pint	¼ pint
Vinegar	¼ ”	—	—
Mustard	½ oz.	½ oz.	½ oz.
Pepper	½ ”	¼ ”	¼ ”
Salt	2 ”	2 ”	2 ”
Potatoes, fresh or	3½ lb.	3½ lb.	2 lb.
Preserved ditto	½ ”	½ ”	½ ”
Water	28 quarts	21 quarts	21 quarts

Food chart for Willis, Gann & Co. from 1855–1857

Illness was rife on some journeys, especially when steerage passengers were confined below decks during massive storms in the Southern Ocean. The ships were cleaned with vinegar and chloride of lime to remove vomit and make things smell better, while precious water was kept for drinking.

Toileting on ships was not pleasant. Often pieces of rag, soaked in vinegar, were hung on the back of the toilet door. These were used to wipe with and were shared over and over, often leading to dysentery! The sewage was often flushed into the bilge with buckets of water until emptied at port. The bilge was below steerage so the stench was not pleasant. People would be horrified these days but back then hygiene was not generally understood.[16]

Emigrant ship, between decks. (London Illustrated News, 17 August 1850)

The sleeping arrangements were bunk beds for steerage, with single women and single men having their own areas. Families often became separated, as most of the time children over the age of 12 were transferred to the single men's or single women's quarters. Bedding was aired in fine weather but often became soaked if water was coming into the ship; this led to influenza and pneumonia outbreaks.[16]

Some ships were better managed than others. The relatively low death count on the *Glentanner's* journeys suggests good management considering the storm they struck, but also some good luck that a major outbreak of illness didn't happen during the journeys.

On the more positive side, a ship journey such as this would have been one of life's biggest adventures for the emigrants. They would see and experience things they never dreamed of, including strange sea creatures, new constellations in the skies and a sea voyage which most would never repeat again in their lifetime, culminating in a strange new land at the final port. At night the passengers entertained each other with music, lectures of the new country and games, made new friends and contacts and looked forward to a brighter future in their new country.

Crew of a Clipper Ship

The average crew of a clipper ship without migrants was about 17, including the Captain, First Mate (or Chief Officer), Second Mate, Midshipman (Apprentice Officer), Ship's Carpenter, Boatswain, 9–10 ordinary seamen and the Cabin Boy who was used for mundane duties. There were usually two cooks: the Passenger's Cook who made food for the steerage passengers; and the Ship's Cook whoc catered for the more refined tastes of the cabin passengers and crew.

The crew numbers were closer to 40 when emigrants were on board, with additional crew including the Ship's Surgeon and Constable to keep the passenger welfare attended to. A Schoolmaster was on board to teach the children and a Matron to separate the single woman from the single men. Sometimes there was also a Minister on board. There were usually several Stewards, who looked after the Cabin Passengers. Some people took up a job on board to get free passage out.[17] The Matron, for example, was often a woman looking to emigrate, who took on the job in exchange for free passage.

Wages for the crew were on average £7 per month on the way to New Zealand with good food and comfortable accommodation but up to £100 wage total for the home journey, to ensure crew stuck with the ship and didn't desert once in New Zealand. Even with the better wage, desertions were common.[17]

The Ship

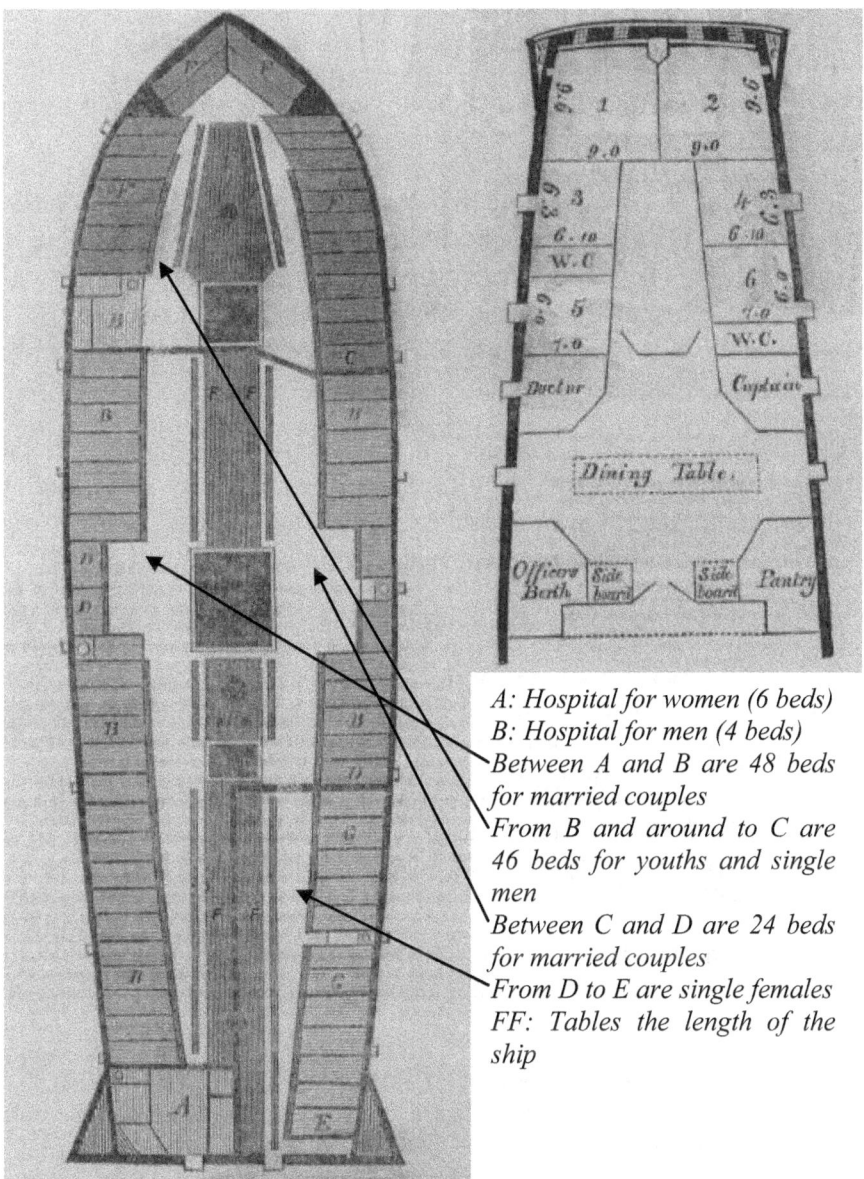

A: Hospital for women (6 beds)
B: Hospital for men (4 beds)
Between A and B are 48 beds for married couples
From B and around to C are 46 beds for youths and single men
Between C and D are 24 beds for married couples
From D to E are single females
FF: Tables the length of the ship

Plan of Emigrant Ship Between Decks (left) and Plan of Cabin Accommodation (right) (courtesy London Illustrated News)

The Recorded Journeys of the *Glentanner*

1843–1844 Voyage from Liverpool to Port Phillip, Melbourne and Sydney, Australia

This voyage is possibly the first long voyage that the *Glentanner* made. The *Glentanner* made this trip as part of a regular line of packet ships. The ship was advertised to leave on about 10 July with passenger fares at a reduced cost. Cabin passengers paid £50; intermediate, £30; and steerage, £20. The agent was Messrs. Fox and Grice, King-street, Liverpool."[18]

The *Glentanner* left Liverpool on 23 August (a bit later than the projected departure of 10 July) and arrived at Port Phillip, Melbourne, Australia on 13 December 1843. The Master was Captain George Brock and passengers as follows:

Mr John Morton, John Gardiner, William Fletcher, Richard Wolfenden, Robert Atkinson, William Kearney, William Kippin, N McLean, Margaret McLean, Henry Stack [Slack][19], Catherine, June, Henry and Elizabeth Stack, Paul, Judith, James, and Mary Phillips, Steerage Aaron, Rebecca John, Sarah Ann and Benjamin Grimshaw, W Kelly, West, Gawthorpe, James Turner, Samuel Charles, William Marks, Colin Hunter, Jane O'Connell, Caroline and Emily Miller, Eliza Lloyd, John Humphrey, Mary and John Wilkinson, JG Giles, Edward Gilbert, John Monk, James Walker, Duncan Menzie, Richard Hethrington, David Johnstone, James Gardiner, David Johnstone, Jane Broadfoot, Robert Frayne, CE Waring, eight Misses McKenna, John McMaster.

Another report gives the passengers travelling from Port Phillip departing 4 January 1844 and arriving 12 January in Sydney as follows:

W. Rearney, John Martin (surgeon), H. Slack. Mary, John, Emma, and Eliza Slack, R. Hitherington, David Johnstone, Robert Thayne, C. E. Waring, John McMaster, and thirteen steerage.[19]

Another report gives the passengers as:

Mr and Mrs Stark with son and 2 daughters, Mrs Langhorne, 2 children and servant, Miss O'Connell, Misses C and E Miller, Miss Lloyd, Messrs R Atkinson, John Morton, Alexander McMaster, Richard Hetherington, David Johnston, Robert Frayne, Charles E Waring, Dare, Kearney, J Turner, S Charles, W Marks, Humphrey, Tysart, Gilbert, Monk, Menzies, Comfort.[20]

The ship was to sail for Valparaiso and Lima on 20 February 1944 with some emigrants, but there had been a falling off in numbers wanting to do this journey. There were doubts that the ship would be allowed to land in Chile, so a deposit was given to the Captain to take them on to Lima or some other part of South America.[21] An advertisement shows how much the passengers had to pay to get to Valparaiso, Chile.

"FOR VALPARAISO DIRECT.
To sail the first week in February
The fine fast-sailing
A 1 British-built ship *GLENTANNER*,

George Brock, Esq., Commander, 610 tons register, only on her second voyage, and from her superior accommodations will be found a first rate conveyance for both cabin and steerage passengers.

Fees for the latter £12, or £5 finding themselves, and as there appears to be an impression that obstacles may be made to their landing by the Chilian Government, a deposit of £5 will be required for their conveyance to some other port should such be the case, but this amount to be refunded should they be allowed to disembark. Apply to the Captain, on board, or to

ROWAND, MACNAB, & CO.,

Harrington-street."[22]

1847 Voyage from London to Sydney, Australia

The *Glentanner* left Gravesend on 4 February 1847 and arrived at Sydney, Australia on 18 June 1847. The *Glentanner* was the Post Office Packet ship (P. O. Pkt.) for February 1847, carrying a very large amount of mail consisting of 4091 letters and 13,500 newspapers. On the journey they spoke no ships that were connected with the colony of Australia.

Passengers were:

Edward John Eyre Lieutenant-Governor of New Zealand; Mrs. Nailor (Naylor),[23] two children, and servant. Mr A. D. Lang. Mr. Gifford, Staff Surgeon Hartwell. Intermediate and steerage:[24] Mr. Thomas and Mrs. Louisa[24] Phillips and son, Mr. Thomas McAuley (Macaulay),[23] Mr. John Jones, Mr. Thomas Bull; and Peri (Piri)[24] Kawau. James Pomari, and George Seelenmeyer, three natives of New Zealand.[25]

The *Glentanner* departed Sydney on 27 July 1847 for Valparaiso, with Captain Brock at the helm; in ballast.[26]

1848 Tender received for the *Glentanner*

On 4 May 1848, an advertisement must have been placed in the United Kingdom for ships to take emigrants to New Zealand. The owner of the *Glentanner*, J. R. Johnston sent a tender in response. It must not have been accepted, however, as it never made a journey to New Zealand until 1857.[27]

Deck of an emigrant ship (Artemisia), The Illustrated London News, 12 August 1848.

1850 Voyage from Plymouth to Sydney, Australia

The *Glentanner* came out yet again to Sydney, this time carrying a "large body of Irish female emigrants." They emigrants, who were apparently Irish orphans,[28] were picked up from Plymouth, but for some reason the ship also went to London. The *Glentanner* scraped her bottom on the way down the Thames and had to dock for repairs before she could set sail into the open ocean.[29] The Irish orphans disembarked and were taken by steamer to a depot on 11 December 1850. Repairs were done. By noon 12 December the emigrants were back on board and by 3 pm she was outside the breakwater and on her way to Sydney. She was repaired very quickly as the ship "convey[ed] important advices to the Cape of Good Hope."[28]

1852 Voyage from China to British Guyana

On 1 September 1852, the *Glentanner* departed from Amoy (Xiamen), China, full of Chinese immigrants. It arrived at Georgetown, British Guiana (Guyana) on 12 January 1853.[30] Other ships that did the London to Lyttelton run, also did a similar trip, including the *Sebastopol,* the *Mystery* and the *Lancashire Witch*.

In 1834, slavery was abolished and the mainly African slaves who had been freed chose to live off the fertile land in British Guyana and take less well paid work, meaning there were fewer workers for the plantations. Sugar plantation owners gained new workers from Portugal, India and some from China. The Chinese workers were mainly travelling under a contract of indenture.

There were 39 ships that brought the Chinese labourers to British Guyana. They were chartered by recruiting agents based in Canton, China, with the cost of shipping shared between the colony's immigration fund and the plantation owners. The ships travelled via Singapore and Cape Town, arriving at Georgetown. The journey usually took between 70 and 177 days.[31]

The *Glentanner* was carrying 305 Chinese but tragically suffered 51 deaths, during the voyage and shortly after arrival. This is a huge death toll. The *Glentanner* was deemed unfit to be an immigrant ship due to lack of ventilation and not enough deck space. However, the Chinese that did start working on the plantations were noted by the plantation owners as being very hard working and cheerful, which made the plantation owners very happy.[32]

An excerpt from a letter written aboard the ship *Mystery* by Rev. William Lobschied on 29 May 1861 gives an insight into some of the passengers on these journeys in general and the state of health they were sometimes in:

"At least two thirds of the men on board were opium smokers ... Men teeming with vermin, full of sores about them, emaciated so as to consist of nothing but bone and skin, scaly and spotted all over from former diseases, three in four full of itch in its most loathsome state, dirty as if they had never seen water, and dull from opium smoking, some of them so weak that they would cry like children when being called to me and wash themselves."

Another passage from the *Royal Gazette* in Guyana of 29 June 1861 stated: "The Ship *Montmorency*, after a passage of 105 days from Hong Kong, arrived here on the afternoon of the 27th instant, assigned to Messrs. Jones and Garnet, with 281 Immigrants of whom 17 were females — a fine, contented batch of people. Seven deaths took place on board and one birth. One of the deaths, as we are informed, was from natural causes, and by others from excessive indulgence in the use of opium. The Captain says that he has been in the habit of carrying English, Irish and Scotch to Australia and that he has much more trouble with them than with this last set of immigrants, who were so peaceable and well disposed that he had no occasion to erect a barricade as usual, and they were permitted to walk about the quarter-deck; ..."[30]

1853 Voyage from Jamaica to Melbourne, Australia

The *Glentanner* arrived in Melbourne on 27 September 1853 from Jamaica, via Bermuda, Bahia and Algoa Bay, with 151 passengers on board.[33] The passengers were described: "many of them highly respectable people, who leave us [Jamaica] merely because they have nothing to do."[34] Many were ruined planters and landowners who were being affected by conditions in Jamaica at that time. The sugar crop in Jamaica was expected to be 35,000 hogsheads in 1853 compared with a production of 200,000 per year previously. Most of the white population was leaving at that time for better pastures.[35]

The *Glentanner* departed Melbourne on 8 May 1854 with Benjamin Bruce at the helm, for Point de Galle, in ballast. No passengers.[36]

1855 Voyage from Plymouth to Sydney, Australia

The *Glentanner* with Captain Benjamin Bruce, and Surgeon S. Hughes, arrived in Sydney on 26 November 1855 with 258 immigrants. There were 76 adult males, 139 adult females, 23 male children, 17 female children and 3 infants. They had an easy passage of 95 days with only one case of measles, from which the patient recovered. Not a single death occurred, but there was one birth.[37] Many of the passengers were "another batch of Irish girls." The paper said: "It really seems as if the Emigration Commissioners never would leave off overwhelming the colony with these unfortunates."[38] The passenger list was:

John and Margaret Brown, Michael and Judy Cormick, Adam, Mar~ garet, Mary, and Lawrence Coleman, James, Sarah, Edward, and James Dedman, William and Elizabeth Dempsey. Edward, Catherine, John and Christopher Flood, Nicholas and Mary Glenen, Alfred, Betsy, and Mary Gully, Michael, Margaret, and John Honan, William, Margaret and John Kent, Cornelius, Margaret and Cornelius Killiber, James and Rebecca Keough, Pat, and Christ, Moran, John and Rosanna Mullan, John and Jane Mackey, Samuel and Mary McKee, John and Mary Nugent, John and Cath. Spencer, Lowry, Jane, and James Stewart, Ellen Byrne, Marianne Blaire, Anne Brady, Cath. Coghlan, Elizabeth Cogney, Charlotte and Emily Campine, Mary Callinan, Mary Callaham, Bridget Carroll, Agness Collins, Bridget Costello, Eleanor Clarke, Cath. Caske, Elizabeth and Maria Cully, Elizabeth Colon, Maria Campbell, Bridget Carty, Mary Cunny, Mary Cook, Bridget and Ellen Downing, Honora Daly, Mary Dooley, Mary Day, Johanna Dooley, Catherine Dixon, Mary Doyle, Margaret Duggan, Ellen Danaghan. Marcella Doyle, Bridget Dondale, Mrs Elliott, Anne and Mary Flood, Alicia Fanning, Bridget Ford, Jane and Sally Fitzpatrick, Anne Farrell, Anne Ferguson, Ellen Friary, Mary Gudy, Letitia Rogan, Mary Hastings, Mary Johnson, Bridget Kane. Johanna Keogh, Sarah Kelly, Elizabeth and Mary Kennedy, Isabella Kelly, Mary Lloyd, Rose and Sarah Lynch, Mary Lyons, Catherine Mackay. Jane Mack, Ellen McCann, Margaret McKone, Alice McCuskie, Sarah Missop, Elizabeth Mills, Agnes Mechan, Sally McClenahan, Fanny McCool, Kate McDonald, Bridget Mullaly, Rose and Jane McGurk, Anne Mellany, Eleanor McCrosey, Anne Owens, Eleanor Rochford, Biddy Rolean, Mary Regan, Mary and Jane Rally, Catherine and Honora Sadler, Mary Spain, Jane and Catherine Sweeney, Mary Sheridan, Mary Tracey, Mary Tucker, Eliza and Agnes White, Jane and Martha

Wilson, John Cohill, John Carr, James Conlon, John Carey, William Doyle, Michael, Patrick, and John Daly, Joseph Donaghy, James Denlin. Joseph Gart, Andrew Graham, Patrick Keane, Willam Kavenagh, Michael Mack, Patrick Elhaton, Noble and Alexander Moore, Daniel McCluskey, Edward McCann Francis Nugent Thomas Owens, Thomas, James, and Grace Tucker, James and Martha Rule, Morris, Mary and James Ahearn, Richard and Elizabeth Bevan, William, Anne, Mary, and David Evans, John, Sarah Eber, Adelaide, Sarah, and Elizabeth Griffiths, Patrick, Elizabeth, John and Catherine Hellernan, Henry, Ellen, and Mary James Esau, Anne, Samuel, Catherine, Daniel, Thomas, Anne, and Jane Jones, John and Ann Jones, Edward, Matilda, Mary, and Thomas Lear, John Jones, Mary, Catherine, John, and Elizabeth Lynch, Patrick, Anne, and John Sullivan, David, Mary, Griffith, William, Deborah, and Thomas Thomas, Richard, Sarah, John, Anne, Ellen, David, Mary, Thomas, Ezekiel, and William Williams, Hannah Charles, Mary Green, Maria and Bridget Griffin, Mary and Anne Molony, Elizabeth Manary, Eliza Morgan, Bridget Stapleton, Mary Smith, Mary and Sarah Thomas, John Clement, Christopher Dent, William Davids, William Fort, Edmund Griffin, Arthur Hogan, John Heweil 2, William Hoare, David and Jeremiah Jenkins, Henry Rezan, John Rees, Michl. Richards, David and Joseph Thomas, and Nathaniel Williams.[39]

1857 Voyage from London to Lyttelton, New Zealand

See the chapter on the first voyage to New Zealand.

1859 Voyage from Southampton to Moreton Island, Brisbane and Sydney, Australia

The *Glentanner* left Southampton on 28 February 1859 and arrived at Moreton Island off the coast from Brisbane, Australia on 5 July 1859 with Captain Wilson in charge and Mr Henry Scott, surgeon.[40] It took 83 days to reach the latitude of the Cape with a total length of passage of 132 days. She didn't stop along the way. She brought in 243 immigrants including 34 single women and 45 single men. They left with 257 immigrants but there was a prevalence of measles and scarlet fever and 23 deaths occurred on the voyage; 4 adults and the rest children. There were nine births. There was also a terrible accident where sailor Thomas Brown, fell from the rigging and died. This event was similar to what happened in 1857 when a sailor was lost in a similar accident. The ship Bremer went to pick up the immigrants and they were ready for hiring in Australia on Monday but many had friends in the district and probably didn't remain locally for jobs. Captain Wilson and Mr Scott the surgeon, both brought their wives out. There was also a Miss Scott, presumably Henry Scott's daughter.[40] Three of the adults who died on board were married men and fathers, and the papers advertised that their families were to be provided for by the "generous public." There was a rumour that the ship met with a sunken rock near the Moreton Island, lighthouse but the newspaper couldn't confirm this.[41]

When the ship was due in port there was a predicament, as detailed in an article from *The Moreton Bay Courier* dated 25 June 1859.

"RUMOUR OF THE *GLENTANNER*.

On Wednesday it was rumoured that this vessel (overdue) with immigrants, had arrived in the Bay on the previous Sunday; and dire was the official commotion. Some of the commentators on public events, who delight to attend to the affairs of the state, were loud in their wail that the newcomers had been so long neglected; one in particular expressing sorrow that the Bachelors' Ball would be interfered with. Official duties called to work, and, consequently, the officers made ready. A nice little party was formed to proceed by the *Bremer*, which had been engaged to convoy the last load to the *British Empire*, previous to her sailing, which was to have taken place on Thursday, but was delayed till yesterday; Captain Haines being also on board of the steam-boat, and the proprietor of this journal; all was, of course, in preparation for properly welcoming the immigrants, and observing due courtesy. Gaily went the steam-boat, having the Custom's boat in tow, and all on board were merry as a marriage-bell. At the depot there was a hurricane. The Agent, it is said, rushed from place to place in frantic haste; then sallied down street to the shopkeepers; much on the praiseworthy principle of Dame Hubbard looking after her dog

He went to a baker's
And bought all the bread,
That those, per *Glentanner*,
Might softly be fed.
He went to a butcher's
And bought all the meat,
Then clear'd out the greengrocers
That dwell in Queen-street.

But mark! The *Bremer* was met by two boats on the river, and the passengers therein informed the officers of the Government that the report was "a sell." The *Bremer* lost her dignity. The custom boat was unfastened, no longer flew the ensign; but the rest of the passengers, save the commander of the custom's boat, went to the Bay. There was no *Glentanner* in the Bay, and shocking to relate, the agent was in a fix to know what to do with the meat, bread, and greens. It is related that the stock-in-trade was inconsiderately cast upon the agent's hands by the tradesmen. What could he do? If he had consumed them himself, he would have needed larger habiliments. The provisions were not exactly the sort for the Bachelors' ball, and it was not dignified to convert the sanctum of red tape into a huckster's store. What the result is, we know not, unless the meat, bread, and greens, are entered as perishable articles. No one can excuse the officers of the Government of not doing what they conceived best; and instead of laughing at the result of the official quickness, we recommended pity for the affair, and the formation of a Joint Stock Company to relieve the agent from his responsibility. The passengers by the *Bremer* returned in good health, feeling a degree of patriotism in having waited to look upon aid rendered to the Vanquish, by lightening her cargo of wheat, brought from Adelaide for Mr. Fleming. The only bad effects of the sell may be, some future time the immigrants may have to suffer through the unbelief of those who will be sceptical, on the plea of, "once bitten twice shy.""[42]

The *Glentanner* departed Morton Bay on 23 August and arrived at Sydney on 31 August 1859 with Captain Wilson, and no cargo. There was one passenger, Mrs. Wilson, the captain's wife.[43]

The *Glentanner* departed Sydney on 12 September 1859 bound for Callao, Peru.[44]

1861 journey from London to Lyttelton, New Zealand.

See the chapter on the second voyage to New Zealand.

The Demise of the *Glentanner*

The *Glentanner* met her demise on the return journey from New Zealand in 1861 with Captain Wilson at the helm. She departed Lyttelton on 4 August 1861, heading for Callao, Peru. Callao was the place for ships to pick up guano for transportation to the United Kingdom. It was a valuable cargo and made the return journey more economic for the owners of the ship.

An interesting article in the North Otago Times, 10 January 1871,[45] talks about the guano trade in the 19th century and what the port of Callao was like. A sailing ship took about six weeks to do the journey from Dunedin to Callao. A massive earthquake in 1630 destroyed the city of Callao and land rose, sunk and was split apart in different places. Then there was another earthquake in 1746 which "swallowed up the city of Callao." Callao had improved in condition as a port since the guano trade had brought wealth to the area.

The Harbour at Callao, c.1866 (Mánuel A Fuentes)

The article says "All vessels are obliged to clear here on their arrival and departure. The streets have been widened, the houses improved, and altogether the town looks well from the bay, though it does not bear a close inspection so well, having all the abominations of South American ports." Numerous vessels crowded the bay. "The harbor generally presents a very lively scene in the number of large and small craft, snuff-colored guano ships, coal ships, steamers, men-of-war, and hundreds of row boats, with white duck awnings, glancing along the placid waters, conveying passengers to and from the shipping."

On one of the Chinchas Islands near Callao, it was estimated in 1850 that there was a depth of 100 feet of guano on the centre of the island gradually decreasing towards the edges, resting on granite underneath. Its main use was for fertiliser for agriculture.[45]

The *Glentanner* made the long voyage over the Pacific Ocean to Callao, Peru. It picked up a load of guano and then travelled around the dangerous Cape Horn, which took many ships to their final grave. However, the *Glentanner* made the trip with no problem, as it had done many times before. They were on their way to Queenstown (not sure which Queenstown) for orders, but on her way up the coast of Brazil, the ship got into trouble. The Irish Times' first reported that the *Glentanner* struck a rock on 2 December 1861 and had become a wreck. The rock was on the Roccas shoal, about 125 miles northeast of Cape São Roque. First reports were that the master and part of the crew were missing, with the mate and eight men arriving safe at Pernambucco, Brazil on 6 December.[46]

A later report states that the other lifeboat landed north of the first lifeboat with the captain and the rest of the crew safe.[47] What a relief! Captain Wilson survived the ordeal.

After so many dangerous trips to Australasia, the *Glentanner* finally met with her watery grave.

Glentanner Advertisements

SYDNEY ROYAL MAIL PACKETS, sailing on the 1st of each month from Gravesend, carrying Her Majesty's mails.—For SYDNEY direct, to sail from Gravesend on the 1st of February, 1847, no goods received on board after the 29th of January, the splendid noted fast-sailing British-built ship GLENTANNER, A 1, 610 tons register, GEORGE BROCK, Commander; loading at the Jetty, London Docks. This fine vessel has a full poop, with spacious accommodations and every convenience for the comfort of passengers, and having good height between decks is well suited for those in the intermediate and steerage. For terms of freight or passage apply to Devitt and Moore, 9, Billiter-street; or to Henry and Calvert Toulmin, 31, Great St. Helen's, Bishopsgate street. The next Sydney packet will sail on February 15, and will be succeeded by the mail packet on 1st March.

The Times (London) 4 January 1847

NEW ZEALAND.——Willis and Co.'s Line of Packets: established 1843.—For CANTERBURY and OTAGO, to sail 31st of May, the fine, first-class, full-poop ship GLENTANNER, Aberdeen clipper-built, 1,000 tons burden, ———, Commander; loading in St. Katharine's Docks. This ship has spacious and well-ventilated accommodation for all classes of passengers, who will be provisioned on a scale of the greatest liberality. A qualified surgeon will accompany the ship. Apply to Arthur Willis, Gann, and Co., 3, Crosby-square, London, E.C.

The Times (London) 18 April 1857

First Voyage to New Zealand

(11 June 1857 – 3 October 1857)

The First Voyage to New Zealand 1857

The *Glentanner* was scheduled to sail on 8 June 1857 from St Katharine's Docks, London.

Arthur Willis, Gann & Co. sent a letter to J. R Godley regarding Godley's comments on their company that were published in the *Lyttelton Times* on 6 December 1856. He basically said that Willis, Gann & Co. were not up to the task of immigration to Canterbury. Godley upset Arthur Willis, Gann & Co. and this prompted them to send a very long letter back. The postscript is of interest though regarding the *Glentanner*. "PS: Since writing the above we have succeeded in fixing the fine ship "*Glentanner*". I intend dispatching her direct to your port in the first week in June – punctually – She is somewhat larger than we intended but we found it impossible to get a smaller ship and we fear we shall find ourselves compelled to disregard your monitions respecting the *Sir Ed Paget* and again repeat the error of sending a vessel to Otago via your Port; we must hope however that you will be able to do better this time."[48]

Quarter deck of an emigrant ship. Mustering of the passengers. (Illustrated London News, 6 July 1850 p.20)

A letter written by T. J. Blackford, sent from Gravesend dated 10 June 1857, stated "At Mr Selfe's request I forward from this place the accompanying statement of assisted Emigrants by the *Glentanner* – with few exceptions the parties are all on board and as comfortable as the confusion consequent on a mass of inexperienced persons first coming into a ship will permit."[49] The passengers would have been mustered at Gravesend and checked over for any diseases, to ensure they were not taken on the ship and spread through the passengers. They would have found their bunk on the ship which was to be their home for the next three or more months at sea.

The *Glentanner* set sail from Gravesend, London on 11 June 1857 with 163 passengers on board bound for Lyttelton, New Zealand. The Captain Benjamin Bruce had never sailed to Australasia and neither had the sailors, except one named Anthony (Augustus in the newspapers) who was described as an "old Portuguese."[50]

The passengers would have settled into ship life fairly quickly. The first part of the journey was usually bad for most, with sea sickness prevalent while in the English Channel, until people found their sea legs. Food allowances were dished out usually on a Monday and church services always on a Sunday. They sometimes had both a Scottish and English service, often held by one of the passengers if no minister was present on board. In between these times the passengers walked the deck, played games (often of their own making), wrote letters home or wrote diaries. If people couldn't write they often got others to write for them. There are no known diaries in existence for the *Glentanner*, only newspaper reports.

Things often became very tedious on such a long journey, but the passengers also had fun times. They saw new constellations in the night sky, amazingly strange animals such as flying fish, and strange islands on the horizon. They often danced and sang at night.

The first two months of the journey on the *Glentanner* the passengers experienced fairly good weather. They had light and variable winds to the equator. After 38 days at sea they crossed the line on 20 July 1857.

They then had pleasant winds until 43 degrees south below the Cape of Good Hope. They were at this position on 18 August. It was from this day that the weather got bad and the trouble began.[51]

On board the *Glentanner* was an eight year old girl Rebecca Doggett who grew up to marry William Bradley in New Zealand. Rebecca lived into her 90s and had vivid memories which never left her, of her journey to New Zealand with her family. Her story was told exactly 80 years later, so presumably there were some errors. For example she calls the sailor named in the newspapers as Augustus Silva, "Anthony". Whether Rebecca was mistaken or the newspaper of 1857 wrong, we may never know. We will call him Anthony in the following account, as per Rebecca's story.[50]

On 20 August, Rebecca remembers the boat being in mid-ocean. The ship had been becalmed for a fortnight with no wind to push it along. They were 3 months out from London, on what was turning out to be quite a long journey compared to the average immigrant ship voyage (usually around 3 months total). The day was hot and calm and there was no sign of an impending storm. The sailors and passengers were dancing on the deck, and Rebecca and her family were below deck celebrating the birthday of her sister Maria. Mrs Doggett had brought a cake in her luggage from England in order to celebrate this special day.[50]

Without warning, the ship was suddenly thrown on its beam ends by a squall.[50] This was at about 7 pm.[51] The ship was literally thrown on its side onto the transverse beams that ran down the deck.[52] At the very least the boat would have been listing 45 degrees, with it possibly being much worse; the masts possibly being almost parallel to the water. The ship would have been about to capsize.[53]

When the boat was thrown, there was a great rattling on the deck and two or three of the dancers tumbled down the hatchway near where Rebecca and her family were. Then, to add to the horror, passenger Mr Craythorne came past them with an iron hook from the rigging through his shoulder.[50]

Captain Benjamin Bruce let out a shout, "My God, we are lost!" and screams and groans from the passengers filled the air with the most terrible noise. It was then that the mainmast head gave way, also the mizzen topmast and jib-boom, which carried away the fore-top gallant mast and the fore-topsail yard. Nearly all the sails were carried away or split, including the fore-topsail, outer and inner and flying jibs, fore and main-top gallant sails, main-topmast stay sail, and cross-jack.[51] Believe it or not, this is what saved them! The ship started to right itself and the captain yelled "No, thank God, we are safe if you men will do your duty quick." [50]

The clipper ship Blackadder (1895) with mainmast and foremast broken. (Attribution Licence 3.0)

The "duty" that Captain Bruce talked about, was to take the rest of the sails down so that the ship wouldn't be thrown over again in the terrifying storm.[51] According to Rebecca, and the story told to her by her mother, it was now pitch dark and the sailors were all too scared to get up on the rigging in the storm. Captain Bruce, who was a fiery Scotsman, was about to get his pistol to make them do it when Anthony (Augustus Silva according to newspapers) offered to do the necessary job if someone would help him. A sailor named Black Sam offered. Anthony was off duty and the captain said he didn't have to go, but Anthony said "Well, our safety depends upon it." [50]

The captain agreed and said, "Yes, and quick too."

While Anthony and Black Sam were up high in what remained of the masts, on the mizzen top-gallant yard[51], part of the rigging and sails came down and Anthony went with them into the sea. It was far too risky and virtually impossible to put out lifeboats and after calling his name and waving torches, no reply came back.[50] Anthony drowned in the ocean – a sad end to such a brave man. He was a hero to all on board!

Black Sam fell down in the same accident but landed on the deck and was badly crushed, but still alive.[50] There is no further information on what happened to Black Sam, but he didn't die on the voyage out to New Zealand. Whether he made it back to England alive is also unknown.

It was the next day before the *Glentanner* could be "got before the wind," being able to only spread her foresail and foretop mast staysail.[54]

For the next two weeks the passengers were battened down inside the ship so that repairs could be made. One can only imagine the monotony and urge to see the sunlight again. When they finally got a look at their ship they saw a very strange sight. Some long spars had been used in place of the full sized masts with some small sails and some rigging attached and the steering gear had all gone.[50] It took them almost another month to limp into the port of Lyttelton, arriving on 3 October 1857. The journey had taken a total of 113 days which was fairly long but thought of as "rapid" considering what had happened to the *Glentanner*.

Births

21 Sep.	Mrs. W. Oliver	a son, died after birth.
02 Oct.	Mrs. W. Robinson	a son.

Deaths

03 Jul.	Jane Hymers	6 months
23 Jul.	James Pringle	16 months

01 Aug.   George Robinson   19 months
20 Aug.   Augustus Silva   able seaman
23 Aug.   William Ivory   12 months
18 Sep.   Joseph Hurdsley (Hardisty?) 8 years.
21 Sep.   Mrs W. Oliver's son   newborn

Passenger Summary

A summary of the passengers was published in the newspapers.

	Adults		Children		Infants	Total
	M	F	M	F		
Cabin	7	4	0	0	0	11
Steerage	75	52	27	23	5	182
Totals	82	56	27	23	5	**193**

	Canterbury	Otago	Total
Chief Cabin	10	1	11
Second Cabin	6	2	8
Steerage	122	22	144
	138	25	**163**

Of the steerage passengers, 90 adults and 34 children were English; 35 adults and 19 children were Scottish; 1 adult and 1 child, Irish; and 1 adult, German, (totals up to **181**).[51] On a quick count of the passenger list in this book the total passengers came to about **184** so at least 9 people are still missing from the passenger list if we take the total of **193** as the final number. The newspaper tables don't seem to add up with each other, and there is no explanation for this.

What did the ship look like before and after the accident?

The following diagram shows the masts and yards of a clipper ship. The masts were usually quite tall. For example the skysail at the top of the Cutty Sark is at 44.5 metres high.[55]

First Voyage to New Zealand 1857

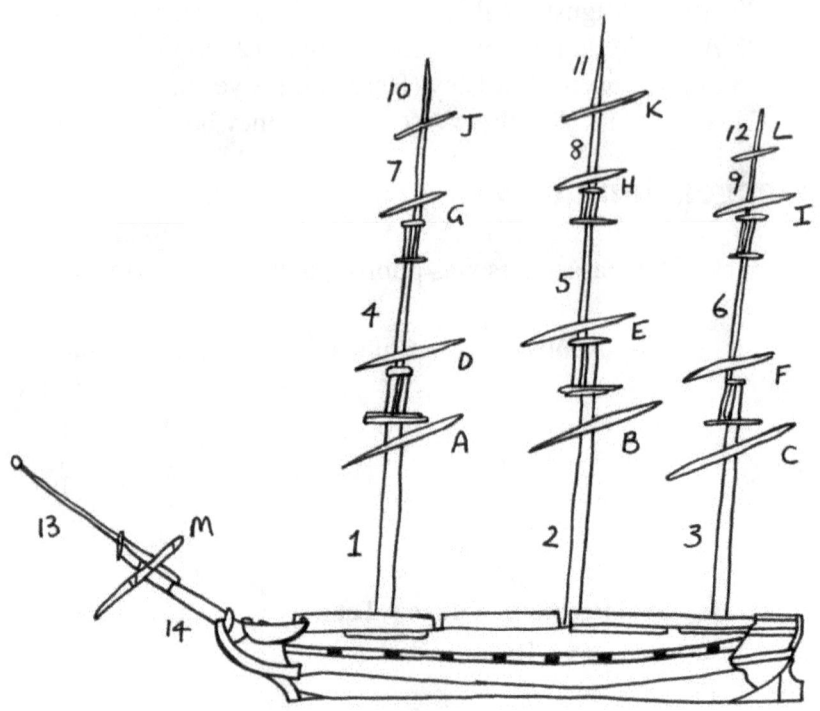

1. fore mast;
3. mizzen mast;
5. main topmast;
7. fore topgallant mast;
9. mizzen topgallant mast;
11. main royal mast;
13. jib boom;

2. main mast;
4. fore topmast;
6. mizzen topmast;
8. main topgallant mast;
10. fore royal mast;
12. mizzen royal mast;
14. bowsprit;

A. fore yard;
C. mizzen yard;
E. main topsail yard;
G. fore topgallant yard;
I. mizzen topgallant yard;
K. main royal yard;
M. spritsail yard.

B. main yard;
D. fore topsail yard;
F. mizzen topsail yard;
H. main topgallant yard;
J. fore royal yard;
L. mizzen royal yard;

The next diagram shows which masts and yards that were lost, according to newspaper reports. It was mentioned that a full mast was broken off short and half of another in some reports,[56] however the initial 1857 report stated which pieces of ship were lost including "the main masthead" which means the top of the main mast.[51] I have done two possible scenarios. One where the main masthead has been removed and one where the main mast is almost completely gone. The fact the mainmast was completely replaced at Lyttelton makes one wonder if it was almost completely lost. Even Captain Benjamin Bruce stated that the full mainmast was replaced.[57]

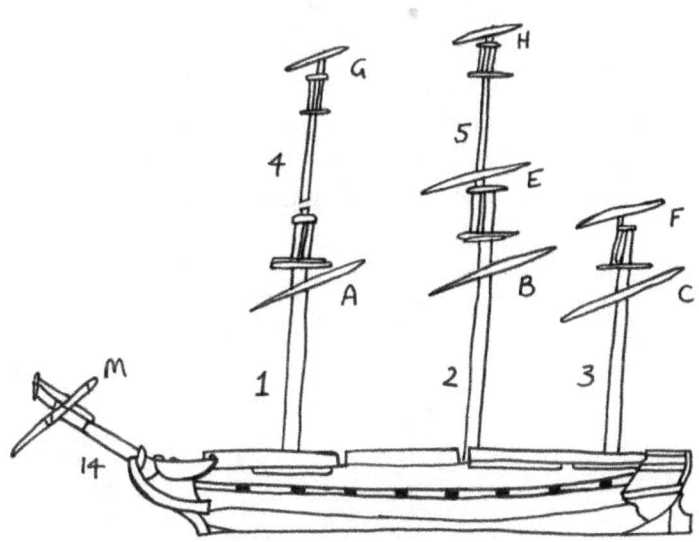

The sailors that died apparently fell from the mizzen topgallant yard, but, according to the papers, this piece of the ship was lost during the storm. Was it lost before the men went up, while they were up there (therefore causing the accident), or after they fell? None of the reports elaborate. In any case, it has been removed in the following diagram, which is an approximation of how it may have looked straight after the accident.

This is the other more dramatic version which is given by passengers such as Charles Oram[56] and Rebecca Bradley.[50]

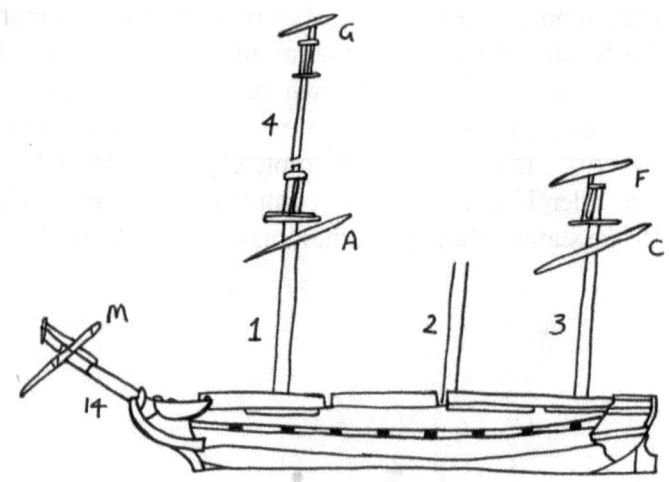

At first the ship could only fly two sails, the foresail and foretop mast staysail. This is what it may have looked like two days after the storm. The carpenter and sailmaker as well as most of the sailors would have been hard at work to make new sails and repair the masts with the new shorter spars available on board.

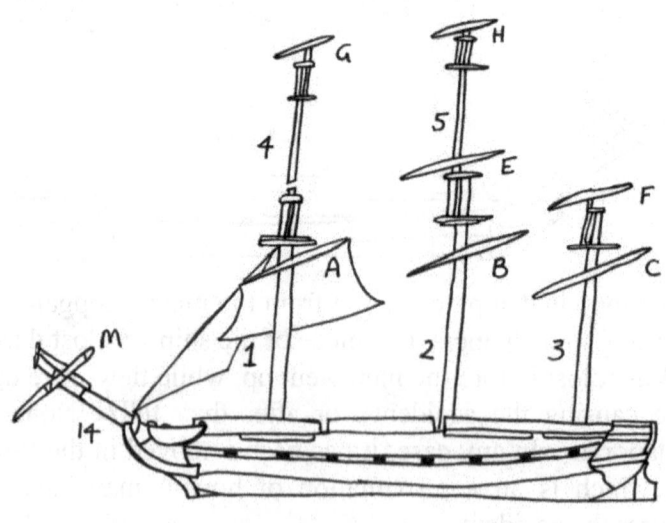

First Voyage to New Zealand 1857

FIRST WOOL SHIP FOR LONDON.
FOR LONDON DIRECT.

THE splendid Aberdeen Clipper built ship GLENTANNER, Captain Bruce, will sail for London direct early in February, having the greater part of her cargo engaged.

Wool shipped by this opportunity has every chance of reaching London in time for the May sales.

The Glentanner has also excellent accommodation for a limited number of passengers.

For freight or passage, early application is necessary to

ROBERT WAITT, & CO.

Norwich Quay, Oct. 16th, 1857.

THE Undersigned, having made arrangements for the ship Glentanner to load wool of the coming clip for London, are prepared to purchase wool and other produce at the highest market rates, or to advance upon the same consigned to their correspondents, Messrs. James Morrison & Co., Philpot Lane, London.

The vessel will afford every convenience for weighing wool on board, and it is confidently expected will be despatched in time to meet the May sales.

ROBERT WAITT, & CO.

Lyttelton, Oct. 15th, 1857.

Lyttelton Times, 26 December 1857

Map of the Journey of the *Glentanner*

First Voyage to New Zealand 1857

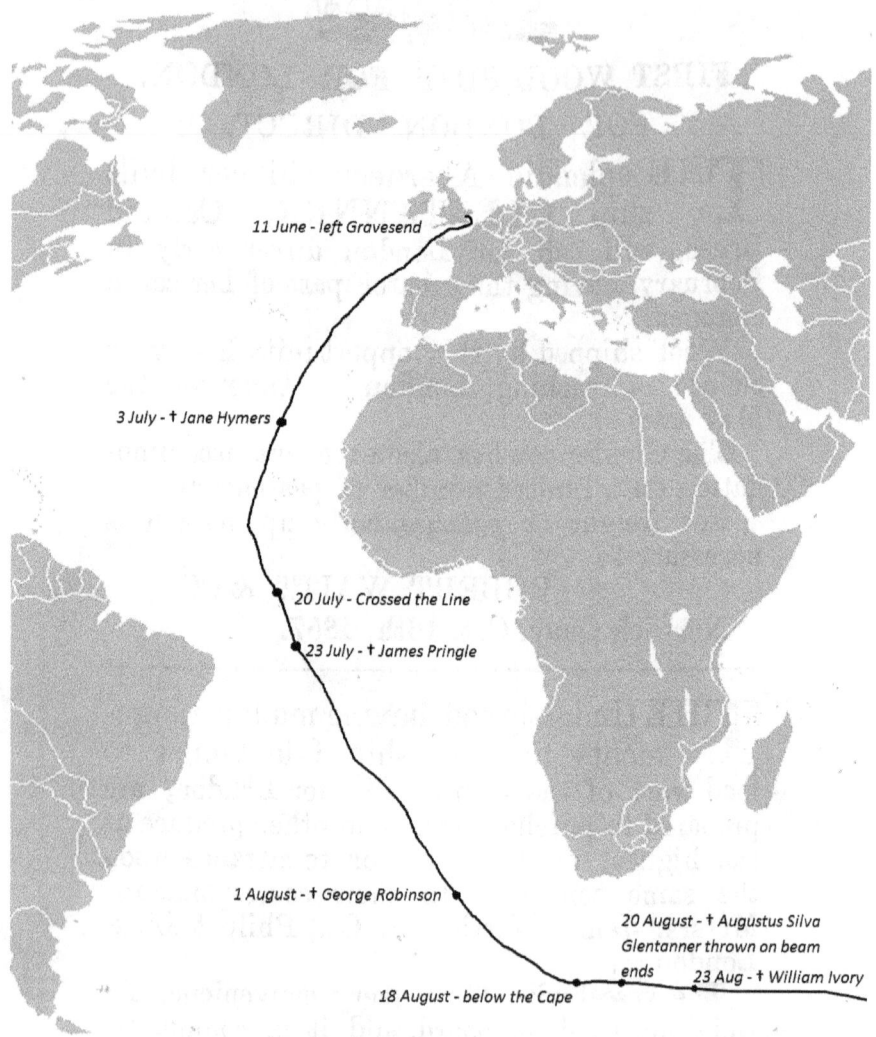

First Voyage to New Zealand 1857

(11 June 1857 – 3 October 1857)

The Arrival of the *Glentanner*

The *Glentanner* was noted in the papers after arrival as being "remarkable as the first accident, worthy of putting on record, having happened to any ship bound from England with emigrants to this port." The accident was noted as being "very nearly fatal" and that, if the masts had withstood the strain, the ship would never have righted itself and been lost at sea with all on board. Most of the people on board were joining friends already in the colony of New Zealand. Apart from the near disaster, the journey was a "prosperous one," with Captain Benjamin Bruce and the officers being kind and with great ability.[58]

The *Glentanner* arrived in Pigeon Bay on 2 November 1857[59] and berthed a little below Sinclair's Bay, (now called Holmes Bay) where she lay while repairs were done. The only difficultly was finding a spar of sufficient thickness for the mainmast. The one found was nearly fifteen feet longer than needed.[60]

A Long Walk

Many of the passengers of the *Glentanner* would have been glad to disembark at Lyttelton and stand on dry land. Many would have had a brief stay the immigration barracks or have been met by family and friends on arrival. Some travelled on to Otago on the *Kate Kearney*. The story of two families after arrival was recorded by Rebecca Bradley, née Doggett, who was eight in 1857.

The Ivory and Doggett families were to be met by William Ivory and William Stapleforth, both relatives already in Canterbury, living in the Rangiora area. The two Williams dined with the two families and they were urged to travel to Kaiapoi where William Ivory would pick them up with his bullock wagon. The two families stayed in the immigration barracks but when they found their luggage would not be sent to Lyttelton for at least two weeks they started out on foot for Kaiapoi. The first trek was over the hill to Christchurch on what was an extremely hot day. One can just imagine the poor women in large skirts and not being able to remove clothing to relieve themselves of the heat. The Ivory family included Aquila, Ann and her sister and their son William. The Doggett family included William and

Matilda with four small girls and a boy. They were carrying a heavy load to make sure the family had enough supplies. Mr Doggett had a large load on his back and also carried his four year old son while Matilda had a basket on one arm and held their youngest, Lucy, aged about one, on the other arm. The young children all carried a parcel each! They made it to Heathcote where they hired a cart to take them to Kaiapoi, stopping in Christchurch for a meal. They made their meal right where the ruins of the Christchurch Cathedral now stand. Then, they took off again for the Waimakariri River. As they neared the river, they saw a Maori Village and the children were frightened. They found the Waimakariri in full flood and the adults were scared to go on the small raft-like punt to Kaiapoi, but the children's fear of the Maori village won out and they decided to trust the punt which got them all over safely. They arrived at Kaiapoi to find William Ivory had left, thinking he had the wrong day to meet them, so it was yet another walk to reach Rangiora. A Mrs Gibbs or Mrs Stone gave them coffee and scones on the way. They got to Edmund Robinson's house and heard the Cam River was in flood and not able to be crossed. A boy took them to a rough bridge and with the help of a few other people they got to William Ivory's place after dark. They were all exhausted from the long trek. The families slept on the floor of William Ivory's small house until they found their own accommodation.

William Doggett bought a property near the Ivory's but died shortly after arrival due to injuries he sustained from an accident back in England. He was buried in the corner of Stapleforth's field.[61]

The *Kate Kearney*

The *Kate Kearney* left Port Cooper (the early name for Lyttelton) and "transhipped" some *Glentanner* passengers to Otago. They were apparently mainly Scottish immigrants. The day they left a heavy gale came up from Banks Peninsula and blew away all the sails! The ship was detained for four days until the weather settled. Then some new sails were unfurled and Captain Dixon managed to do the journey to Otago and back in fourteen days.[62] Passengers for Otago were Brugh and Henderson and 20 in steerage.[63]

The *Glentanner* Repairs

Benjamin Bruce wrote a letter to the editor of the *Lyttelton Times* to praise the port of Lyttelton for having masts and spars suitable for the *Glentanner*, in order for her to be repaired. They found lengths of 20 to 65 feet in length, which quite surprised for him.[57]

The *Glentanner*'s hull was undamaged after close inspection but her masts and spars were very badly damaged. Fresh spars were easily at hand, despite Canterbury having bare plains. The repairs were also completed in a very fast manner, allowing her to make her journey home, full of wool. The *Glentanner* was chartered as one of the season's wool ships. Because of the repairs and the ship staying in port, this meant that the wool could be loaded directly from coasting vessels without being landed, warehoused and reloaded. The loading of wool was far better for the colony than ships proceeding in ballast to India or China, which seemed such a waste.[64]

The *Glentanner* travelled back into Lyttelton Harbour from Pigeon Bay on Thursday 31 December, as her refit had been completed.[65]

The *Lyttelton Times* had a large editorial written on the repairs of the *Glentanner*. Most of the labour was supplied by the ship's crew and the locally-supplied mainmast and fore top mast were much cheaper than anything available in England, if not of slightly "inferior dimensions." The fact that the Port of Lyttelton had the ability to find materials and repair ships must have come as a surprise to many of the locals. The Editor of the *Lyttelton Times* wanted to highlight how great it was that this job had been done with ease in such a small settlement.[66]

Glentanner Station

The Dark brothers, Cornelius and Edward were supposedly on board the *Glentanner* in 1857 but were not listed on the passenger list. They took up a Run in 1858 and called it Glentanner Station after the ship.[67] They apparently first settled in Nelson, building cob houses before going to the Mackenzie Country. It was sometimes called

"Old Dark's run." There was bush on the run, which was very rare for the Mackenzie Country and kea used to live in the bush there.

The Dark brothers sounded like hard cases. They hated tourists from England coming down to see Mt Cook and expecting to stay at their run (there was no Hermitage in those days). They tried to be nice to them but once some visitors were put up in a fled infested hut, which of course didn't go down too well.

Edward Dark had feuds with his neighbours including Dawson of Ben Ohau. Dark practiced before an impending fight once, on a sack of flour hung from the rafters of the station hut. After a few punches, Dark was no longer dark but white. Dawson, who was younger, won the fight despite Dark's practice.

Edward Dark or "Old Dark," as he was known, cleaned his shirt in a hurry one day by washing it in a stream. He then mounted his horse and tied the shirt around his own shoulders so it flew in the breeze and dried as he rode to the Timaru cattle show in a hurry.

Cornelius Dark died in 1882 and "Old Dark" sold out to the Thompson brothers in 1883.[68]

Those who didn't sail

There were many people listed at the beginning of the original passenger list for the *Glentanner* who decided not to sail on the *Glentanner* for various reasons.

John Cracroft Wilson was a settler and landowner in Christchurch and had a property he called *Cashmere* at the Port Hills.[69] John had employed some shepherds and was shipping them to New Zealand aboard the *Glentanner*. However, they came on the ship *Maori* instead.

Margaret Cotton and six children had already left for New Zealand, on the *Maori*. Lucy Huntington had two sponsors trying to get her to New Zealand but she declined going out. No reason was mentioned. George Prebble, wife and 5 children had notice of their sponsored passage to New Zealand sent twice, but they never boarded, for a reason unknown.[70]

The Regatta

The *Glentanner* took part in the Lyttelton Regatta held on 2 January 1858.[71] The regatta was going to be held on New Year's Day, but the weather was bad so was postponed until the next day with shops closing to mark the event.

The Lyttelton Time stated, "The harbour was very gay. Besides the fleet of coasting craft which had come into port for the occasion, the *Glentanner, Bosworth*, and *Oriental* were present, and made an agreeable addition to the appearance of the water. All vessels were dressed in a suit of flags; and those just named, with the Corsair schooner, kept the harbour alive, firing in answer to the guns from the shore, and in salute to the racing craft which passed by them."

All races started from the jetty and the boats had to sail out to the *Glentanner*, tack around it and return towards the flag boat out from the jetty. Captain Bruce sailed an open boat under 4 tons in a race against two other boats, but according to the papers the small *Glentanner* boat kept the lead and won "as was to be expected from a boat of her qualifications."

As well as the boat races there were also onshore activities for the general public who didn't sail. The report on these activities is quite amusing: "The shore sports came just before the duck hunt. Sorry as we are to cast a damp upon any amusements which endeavour to flourish among us, we must confess to being thoroughly disgusted with such ridiculous amusements as were those of Saturday afternoon. The greasy pole displayed some gymnastic power in the boy who succeeded, but we should have much preferred the exercise without the grease; and the jingling match was certainly the poorest attempt at amusement we ever witnessed; the red nightcaps were the only attractive part. No footraces, jumping (except in sacks), nor wrestling, were thought of. We hope on another occasion to witness some competition in some sports wherein a man may pride himself in excelling. The fun was not over till half-past eight p.m., after which the town was quiet."[71]

Glentanner Cargo 1857

In the Glentanner, R., Latter, agent; 46 cases, 117 casks, 20 kegs, 33 hhds., 1 tierce, 2 chests, 1 bale, 15 jugs and baskets, 5,000 slates, 130 tons coals, 400 bags salt, 77 boxes soap, R. Latter; 10 cases, Campbell & Co.; 5 brls. ale, 5 cases, Cookson, Bowler & Co.; 17 bales, 23 cases, 21 crates, 15 casks, 30 boxes, 4 firkins, 4 tierces, 4 kegs, 2 sheets lead, Gould & Miles; 15 hhds. 10 brls. beer, Tomlinson; 18 cases wine, Kennaway; 30 pckgs. (house) Morgan; 2 hhds. wine, Aikman; 11 cases, Waitt & Co.; 1 case, Field; 1 pckge. Martin; 1 case, Gee; 1 box, Coyte; 1 box, Frost; 1 box, Worsley; 1 box, Balestiee; 1 box, Wormald; 2 cases, Basham; 1 box, Curlett; 1 case, Yule; 1 case, Neagle; 2 casks, Gresson; 2 cases, Williams; 1 cask, Phillips; 1 case, Mackie; 1 case, Raymond; 1 case, Horncastle; 7 pkgs., 1 case, 4 wheels, 1 carriage, 1 axle, 1 pair shafts, 1 box, C. J. Perceval; 1 case, Hanmer; 1 box coin, H. Miles; 102 pkgs. for Otago.

The Lyttelton Times, 10 July 1857

The Departure of the Wool Clipper *Glentanner*

The *Glentanner* departed Lyttelton Harbour for London on 6 April 1858 with Captain Benjamin Bruce at the helm. There were two passengers on board, Mr. E. Phillips and Mr. T. Hill.[72] The ship was noted to be "as full as an egg with wool." The ship *Oriental* was also full of wool and left a few days behind the *Glentanner*.[73] The *Glentanner* hoisted the last bale up to the yard-arm while the crew cheered. This happened on Thursday 1 April 1858.[74] So many trials and then the job was done and they were going home!

The *Glentanner* and the *Oriental* arrived at London on 30 July 1858, together, delivering their wonderful cargoes of New Zealand wool.[75] The *Glentanner*'s cargo was worth £45,000 and the *Oriental* £35,000, making the year's exports the biggest ever for Canterbury to that date.[76]

Captain Bruce's Fight

Benjamin Bruce was the Master of the *Glentanner* from 10 April 1854, when he was appointed to the position by the owners at that time, Messrs. Hyde, Hodge and Co. of London. The ship was in Melbourne at the time of his appointment.

He travelled to Lyttelton in 1857 and endured the storm that nearly sunk the *Glentanner*. Captain Bruce received his payment on arrival in Lyttelton. While in New Zealand, Captain Bruce had to borrow £400 7s. 5d from Messrs. Waite and Co. as he had run out of money for running the ship. He arrived home to the London Docks on 1 August 1858. In the meantime Hyde, Hodge and Co. sold the ship to Messrs. Vaughan and Co., who took possession on 7 August 1858.

Hyde, Hodge and Co. went bankrupt and Captain Bruce was left with a debt of £400 7s. 5d, which should have been paid by the owners, but Vaughan and Co. refused to pay.

After a lot of fighting between parties, the judge came to the conclusion that the new owners should pay this amount and why should the Master of the ship be liable for the amount.

Poor old Benjamin Bruce managed to get himself out of owing money before leaving as Master of the ship.[77]

There was another problem with the ship owners going bust, which included the crew not being paid what they were owed.

Benjamin Bruce also had to go to court to fight for his crew's wages. This was for 18 crew members, who had asked for various amounts to be paid to them. The men had apparently been promised double the wage for the trip home whilst they were at Lyttelton by Captain Bruce. The ship owners considered the seamen were under the contract they signed back in London. Because the judge considered the men had been misled and had false hopes of double the wage, he ordered they be paid their wages owing plus £10 each (apart from two crew members who did not enter into the new contract; they got one guinea costs paid to them).

The crew members involved in this court case were:

David Birt	£35 81s
Edwin Stace	£32 14s 6d
James Bamfield	£32
Charles Sullivan	£34 10s
William Pearce	£33
Alfred Perkins	£32
Alexander Hamilton	£33 10s
Samuel Williams	£45 14s
John Purdy	£50
William Thompson	£31 10s
J. F. Bohemnn	£22 10s
Frederick Groves	£19 10s
Richard Gardner	£30 5s
John Humphreys	£31
Henry Greenhill	£9 7s
Frederick Sherry	£19 15s
Alfred Randall	£33
Charles Crispin	£13

The article on crew wages from 31 December 1858 stated: "Mitchell's Maritime Register, August 21. Messrs. Hyde, Hodge & Co. owners of the *Glentanner*, stopped payment in the beginning of August [1858]. Their assets are stated at about £75,000, and liabilities not less than £185,000, A meeting of creditors was held on August 14, at which it was resolved to wind up the estate under inspection."[78]

Glentanner Reunions

The *Glentanner* went through a rough journey, with the passengers being lucky to be alive, and this would have brought them closer together. In 1897 they had their first recorded reunion. Some immigrant ships had no reunions.

The 1897 reunion was the fortieth anniversary and was celebrated at Hawker's Hall in New Brighton, Christchurch where they had a luncheon.[79] Forty invitations were sent out and thirty made the reunion. Mr R. D. Thomas was Chair and Mr W. Bush was the Vice Chair. There were many happy speeches from them. Mr W. Bush, Miss Bush and others sang songs, with Miss Bush as pianist. When the ages of the 17 men present were added up, the total came to 945 years. They left the ladies' ages alone!

Ward Robinson was the oldest at 78 years old and Daniel Day was about 74, just behind him. The youngest was Harry Fielder, who was 46 years old. He travelled down from Wellington for the reunion.

There were a lot of reminiscences told including "adventures by flood and field"[80] and the group of shipmates returned to town at about 5.40pm.[81]

Mr R. D. Thomas was presented with a solid silver salver, by his shipmates, to thank him for organising the reunion. He gave thanks and said that it would always be treasured by him and his wife as a memento of the *Glentanner* reunion.[82]

In 1902 there was another reunion of passengers. Edwin Parnham of Beachvale, Kaiapoi, organised the reunion and was presented with a "handsome" silver basket inscribed "To Edwin Parnham from his fellow passengers by the ship *Glentanner* (October 1857) in appreciation of the reunion at Kaiapoi, October 3rd, 1902."[83]

The next reunion was the 50th anniversary held on 3 October 1907. George McRae who organised the reunion, was not in great health on the day of the reunion, so others officiated. The photo on the next page was taken in front of Cave Rock. It is poor quality due to being copied from a dark image on the microfiche in the Christchurch Public Libraries.[84]

Names synonymous with the *Glentanner* were: Mr Colborne Veel, the Boags, Mr. R. D. Thomas, the Oram brothers, George McRae and Edwin Parnham, as well as many others, who were known as old colonists who laid the foundations for New Zealand.[84]

This photo was published in the Canterbury Times, 9 October 1907 with the following notes underneath:

"THE JUBILEE OF THE ARRIVAL OF THE SHIP *GLENTANNER*"

The jubilee (1857-1907) of the arrival of the ship *Glentanner* at Port Lyttelton was celebrated at the Cafe Continental, Sumner, on October 3. Twenty-seven passengers and their wives assembled at the invitation of Mr George McRae of Ashburton. Mr E. Parnham presided, with the host on his right. Mr. W. Bush occupying the vice-chair. After a sumptuous luncheon, the chairman, in a very happy speech, proposed the health of the host, which was enthusiastically honoured. The toasts of the chairman, the honorary secretary (Mr. F. C. East) and the ladies were also honoured and duly responded to. The party was then photographed, and members afterwards recounted interesting reminiscences of the voyage out in the old ship. The following are the names of the passengers of the *Glentanner* who met at Sumner. Standing, from left to right – Mrs Kimber, Mr T. Dawson, Mr A. East, Mr F. W. East, Mr E. Parnham, Mr G. McRae, Mrs Fielder and Mrs Johnstone. Sitting – Mrs Weavers, Mr W. Bush, Mrs Rutledge, Mrs King, Mr W. Evans and Mr T. Bradwell."[85]

The next year (1908) it was reported that "fifty-one years ago today [3 October] the ship *Glentanner* (Captain Bruce) dropped anchor in Lyttelton harbour. There are about thirty or forty of the passengers remaining in Christchurch."[84]

Passengers on the 1857 Voyage

Passengers on the 1857 Voyage

Allen

Martha Allen was listed as only 14 when she travelled on the *Glentanner* to New Zealand. She was going to travel with Joseph Allen (aged 16), who was probably her brother, but he never boarded as the passenger list said "absent from England." She was sponsored out by Robert Allen (likely a relation) and E. Dobson.

Barton

Henry Albert Barton was 20 when he travelled out on New Zealand on the *Glentanner* in 1857. He lost luggage after arrival.

> LOST, OR MISLAID.
>
> A BAG and a BOX with the name of H. BARTON, per Glentanner, for Port Lyttelton, and which was landed on the 7th of October. Whoever has found the same is requested to leave them at 'Mr. SALT'S, London street, Lyttelton, or Mr. DANN'S Store, Christchurch.

Lyttelton Times 4 November 1857

At age 23 he married Amelia Mercy Pratt in 1859 in Christchurch.[86] They had a daughter Amelia Ann in 1860. Amelia Barton then appears in 1877 as a brothel owner in Timaru who was charged with selling alcohol without a licence. Sadly she kept her daughter there as a prostitute. Amelia was sent to prison for two months.[87] What happened to Henry, is unknown as a death cannot be confirmed for him. Amelia Mercy Barton died in 1897 aged 55 and was buried in Geraldine Cemetery.[88] The daughter, Amelia Ann Barton, married James Coppell in 1908 aged about 48. They probably had no children. Amelia Ann Coppell lived until 1932.[89]

Boag

William and Jane Boag travelled with their children on the *Glentanner*. Their son, John Boag was born in Perthshire, Scotland in 1841 and was brought up on a farm. He came to New Zealand on the *Glentanner* in 1857 and bought Crown land in 1865, calling the property *Middlerigg*. John also bought 900 acres of freehold land on the Rakaia. He had a large two-storey house and a plantation of trees, plenty of good fences and outbuildings. John Boag was on the local road board and school committee, and was President of the Ellesmere Agricultural and Pastoral Association. He married Grace Stewart[89] in 1865 and they had three sons and two daughters.[90] John died in 1925 and Grace in 1931.[89]

Mrs. J. Cunningham

Anne Boag, sister to John, who was 19 when she travelled out with her parent,s married John Cunningham in 1862 and moved to Brookside, which was then known as South Selwyn. Anne was a great pioneering woman, handling the hardships of early life in New Zealand very well. She was known for her hospitality and gave many meals to those in the area prospecting for land. They lived in a sod␣whare in the early days and would offer people a bed for the night in this very basic house. They had two sons and two daughters.[91] John and Ann retired to Christchurch 14 years before she died in 1916.[92]

Mr. J. Boag

Bradwell

Caroline Bradwell came out to New Zealand on the *Glentanner,* with two children, Albert, aged 10 and Caroline, aged 7, to meet up again with her husband Albert Thomas Wardle Bradwell. He was a printer residing in Christchurch. Albert gave evidence in an assault case in 1863 when he heard a man being hit and then strangled in the dark.[93] They had another child, Annie Lyttelton Bradwell, in 1867.[89] In March 1870, the family lived in Colombo Street and Albert was a newsagent.[94] Albert died in October 1870 aged 52 and Caroline died in 1898 aged 75.[89]

Brooks

Henry and Elizabeth Brooks had at least five more children after arriving in New Zealand on the *Glentanner*, four girls and a boy, swelling their family to eight. One child was Charles George Osborn Brooks, who was born in 1861 and baptised in 1863 in Christchurch. The witnesses were fellow *Glentanner* passengers John and Elizabeth Hodgson. Henry was listed as a Barrack warden residing in Lyttelton. This was probably the Lyttelton Immigration Barracks.[86]

Brugh

Sheddan Brugh was one of the cabin passengers on the *Glentanner* who was bound for Otago. He was an engineer on a troopship during the Crimean War. His parents were the first settlers of the Catlin area and were farmers. Sheddan followed in their footsteps. For the last 20 years of his life he travelled the world extensively. Sheddan died in Dunedin in 1915 aged 85.[95]

Bush

William Bush was born in Great Dunmow, Essex, England in 1834. He arrived at Lyttelton on the *Glentanner* in 1857 and had a house-decorating business there for many years. He was very interested in the progress of the city as it developed, and he collected photos of the pioneer and pilgrim settlers. He presented this collection to the Christchurch Museum in January 1895. It is now of great historical value.[96] He died in 1910. Many of his shipmates attended his funeral at Barbadoes Street Cemetery, as did members of the Veterans Cricket Club and other friends.[97] William Bush had a daughter, Miss M. E. Bush, who was a pianist and vocalist.[98]

Mr. W. Bush

Chappell

Edwin Stone Chappell came to New Zealand on the *Glentanner*, aged only sixteen. He married Mary Sullivan in 1865.[89] Edwin lived at Long Bay Road, Akaroa in the 1870s.[99] There were a series of court cases involving the Chappell and Jones families of Akaroa. Mary Chappell was charged with assault and abusive language. E. S. Chappell was charged with threatening language and attempting to rescue cattle. The Jones family were charged by the Chappell family in return.[100] Hopefully they sorted the neighbourhood feud after a day in court. Edwin Chappell died in 1927 aged 86.[89]

Clement

William Henry Clement was born in Somersetshire, England and at age six travelled to New Zealand with his parents on the ship *Glentanner*. His father, Shadrack Clement, bought land at New Brighton, which he farmed for many years. William moved away to Tekoa station in North Canterbury and started his own 1200 acre farm at Mayfield. In 1889, he took on a lease for 433 acres from the Government. He partially cleared the land of stones and cultivated it, sewed grass and had two sheep to the acre. Some of his trees were forty feet high in 1903. William married Annie Elizabeth Austin in 1885[89] and they had three sons and four daughters.[101] William died in 1908. Shadrack Clement died in 1914, aged 82.[89]

Colborne-Veel

Mr Joseph Veel Colborne-Veel was born in 1830 in Gloucestershire. He was educated at Kidderminster and Magdalen Hall, Oxford where he gained an M.A. in 1856. In 1857, Joseph and his wife (Anne Maria Anstey, of Oxford) came to New Zealand on the *Glentanner*. They married at St John's, Notting Hill, London, just before leaving on the ship. Mr Veel was editor of *The Press* from 1861 to 1878. He resigned to become secretary of the North Canterbury Board of Education. At

Mr. Colborne-Veel

Oxford, when he was young, he was known as a light-weight athlete and in older years he loved chess. Mrs Colborne-Veel had been an invalid for many years before dying in 1910. Joseph died before her in 1895.[102] When he died he had one son and three daughters.[103] One of their daughters Mary Caroline Colborne-Veel became a well-known Christchurch poet.[104]

Craythorne

William Craythorne travelled on the *Glentanner* to New Zealand and survived the ordeal, despite having an iron hook go through his shoulder during a squall.[50] He came with his wife Mary and four children. He became a farmer, residing in Lincoln Road, Christchurch.[105] In 1865, he had an alcohol license for Lincoln Road and Halswell Junction.[106] After William's death at age 54 in 1872,[89] the Rangiora Brewery, which he had a share in, was put up for sale.[107] In 2013, Craythorne's Public House (Est. 1863), is in Halswell, probably on the site of William's first public house. It used to be called the Halswell Tavern.[108] Mary Craythorne died only a few months after William, aged 55.[86]

Dark

Glentanner station was first taken up the Dark Brothers in 1858, after they arrived on the *Glentanner* in 1857. They named the station after the ship. The Dark brothers, Edward and Cornelius, are not listed on the official passenger list or in the newspapers as being cabin passengers. *Glentanner* station was 60,000 acres in size.[67] Cornelius Dark died in 1882, a sheep farmer from *Glentanner* Station, MacKenzie Country, aged 54. He died in Christchurch Hospital. He was buried in Barbadoes Street Cemetery, Christchurch. His next of kin was listed as William Dark.[86] It is unknown what became of Edward Dark.

Dawson

Thomas Dawson was born at Macclesfield, England in 1834. He worked as a labourer until he emigrated to New Zealand on the *Glentanner*. His future wife, Harriet Holmes, who he married in 1860, was also a passenger, travelling with her parents. After arriving, Thomas worked in Riccarton for Thomas Rawley, and later bought a farm in Hanson's Road. He then bought the old *Cabbage Tree Farm* of 58 acres at Hornby, which he farmed until 10 years before his death. At first, the Dawsons lived in a mud house on the farm. He built a little wooden lean-to and then added on to the house over the years until there was a double storey. When Mr Dawson first arrived, there were only three houses making up the village of Hornby. He was a member of the Templeton Anglican Church and a founder of St Columba's Anglican Church at Hornby, for which he donated the land it stands on. The font in the church was given by Thomas in memory of his wife. Thomas was very involved in the local community of Templeton and Hornby in general. Harriet Dawson died in 1902 and was buried at Riccarton Churchyard. They had a family of four sons and three daughters. On Thomas's death in 1924, age 90 years, he had twelve grandchildren and seventeen great grandchildren.[109]

Day

Daniel Day was born in Somersetshire, England in 1823. He was a bricklayer before travelling to New Zealand on the *Glentanner* with his wife, son and daughter. He started working for Messrs Washbourne Bros and built their first wooden homestead. Daniel bought ten acres of land at Ladbrooks, later adding 20 acres to it. After holding it for seven years before selling, he made a big profit and was able to buy about 203 acres in Springston. It was totally unimproved and needed a lot of work, but the hard work paid off for him. He retired in 1870 and leased his farm to his son-in-law. Daniel then lived in Lincoln Road at Somerset Cottage, and would use a bicycle despite his age (1903).[110]

Mr. D. Day

Didcock

Esther Didcock married Henry Thomas William Carter in 1858 after arriving on the *Glentanner* in 1857. They had at least six children.[89]

Dobbs

Mrs Rebecca M. Dobbs, a nurse and widow, from Queens County, Ireland, was brought out to New Zealand by Henry Dobbs and George Dobbs, who were likely relations of hers. There was a Joseph Manning Dobbs, age 10, in the single men's quarters and he is likely related to Rebecca.[70]

Doggett

The Doggett family who came out on the *Glentanner,* were related to the Ivory family. Their daughter, Rebecca Dogget,t grew up to marry William Bradley, and her memoirs told the story of the family travelling to Rangiora to start their new life. They were a pioneer family of Rangiora.

East

Frederick Charles East was born in Oxford, England and came to New Zealand on the *Glentanner* with his mother and brothers. He is not, however, on the passenger list. In his mother's obituary it says that Frederick "subsequently" came to New Zealand, so there is some confusion here. Frederick was a member of the Volunteer Company in Canterbury. Frederick worked for the *Lyttelton Times* Company and then became a draughtsman. He became head of the proof-reading staff. He was a fine horseman and in 1862 rode Mr. H. P. Lance's Azucena, the winner of the second Derby run in Christchurch. He was also a musician and photographer, and took many valuable pictures of Christchurch that became historic. He took some of the first photographs published in the Canterbury Times. Frederick was also an excellent horticulturalist and won many prizes at shows. His collections of ferns, palms and orchids were some of the finest in New Zealand. Frederick died in 1916 at the age of 71.[111]

Frederick's brother, Herbert E. East became a Reverend at St. Mary's Addington and then lived at Leithfield. His other brother A. E. P. East lived in Merivale.

His oldest brother was Mr. F. W. East of Prebbleton, known as Frank, who died a few months before him. Frank took part in the

"Gabriel's Gully rush" and spent about a year looking for gold, quite unsuccessfully. He then tried the Greymouth goldfields with the same bad results! He started a threshing machine plant back in Canterbury and owned a traction engine, which was much more successful. In 1882 Frank was made clerk of the Lincoln Road Board and in 1902 was Register of Electors for the district of Courtenay. He was a member of the Lincoln Lodge. He cultivated hyacinths and narcissi, and had one of the best collections in the district. He married Miss Monk, niece of Andrew Dawson of Longbeach, and they had one son and two daughters.[112]

The boys' mother, Mrs Sarah East, left England in the hope of offering her sons good opportunities in New Zealand. All her sons got excellent positions including F. C. East who (according to her obituary) had subsequently arrived in New Zealand. She married Antill Alfred Adley in 1860. She bought land on Colombo Street and, with her new husband, built the Oxford Hotel, which they managed for several years and then leased. Sarah was living at Opawa when she died in 1890. She was always working for the good of the neighbourhood, including her local churches. She "commanded great esteem" in her local parishes. Sarah had a son to Mr Adley named Cecil Antill Adley. She passed away at the age of 73 and was buried in Heathcote cemetery.[113] What a wise and brave woman she was to take a huge journey to New Zealand to help her sons.

Fielder

Henry V. Fielder arrived on the *Glentanner* in 1857 and started business as a picture frame maker and gilder on the corner of Armagh and Colombo Streets. He then built the Garrick Hotel, where he lived for a short time before moving to Kilmore Street where he lived for about thirty years. He passed away in 1894. He was "greatly respected by all who knew him."[114]

Henry Fielder junior, was born in London, England and came to New Zealand with his parents on the *Glentanner*. He made furniture with his father for many years and then moved to Wellington in 1868. He established his own furniture business in 1880 in Manners Street. He then took over the Family Hotel at Lower Hutt, which he was licensee of at the time of his death at age 63 in 1915. He had two marriages.[115]

Forbes

William Forbes was only 16 when he migrated to New Zealand. He was born in 1839 and christened in Nether Banchory, Aberdeenshire, Scotland.[116] He was going to travel with his mother and step-father Charles and Mary Paterson née Anderson, but they decided not to travel on the *Glentanner*. Instead they made their way to New Zealand in 1860 on the *Matoaka* with five other children. Jane Forbes, William's sister, was also going to travel to New Zealand but ended up marrying James Milne in Scotland and producing nine children.[117] William Forbes worked as a groom and bullock driver in the Kaiapoi/Ashley area.[118] He married Ann Anderson in Kaiapoi in 1863 and they had 5 children but only three lived to adulthood. Their names were John, Ann, George Henry, Frances Charles, and James Hary. William owned land in Waipara. He also had land at Salt Water Creek in partnership with two others. The same 3 men also ran the Weka Pass Accommodation House, which was a place for goldminers to stay when trekking to the West Coast. Later, William and Thomas Henry Evans had a partnership running the City Hotel, Leithfield.[116] William died at a young age of tuberculosis, at his residence in Balcairn in 1877.[119]

William Forbes

Galletly

Peter Galletly travelled with his wife, Marjory, three year old son John, and an infant, aged 7 months. They had at least four more children in New Zealand: Peter, born 1861; Margaret, born 1863; Ann, born 1865; and Mary, born 1872.[89] Peter Galletly owned land near Leeston Railway Station. The land caught on fire in 1869 and burnt a great deal of grass on the Run belonging to Mr Cracroft Wilson. A court case ensued and Peter was charged 100 pounds in damages.[120] Peter died in 1875, aged 44 residing in Templeton. Marjory died two years later in 1877 at the same age of 44 years.[86] There was a Peter Galletly who escaped from Sunnyside Lunatic Asylum in 1884 and 1885. He was in his twenties, so was possibly Peter and Marjory's son. He was described as about 5 foot 8 in height with dark hair and grey eyes, and was deaf and dumb. In 1884, he was wearing a suit of white moleskins and a straw hat.[121] In 1885 he was heading for Templeton wearing the same white moleskin trousers and a tweed jacket.[122]

Peter's brother, David Galletly, was also on the *Glentanner* in the single mens' quarters. He became a farmer and married Ann Norfolk in 1861.[86]

Grant

John Grant was born on Christmas Day in 1825 in Crumble, Strathspey, Scotland.[123] He and his wife and two children travelled to New Zealand on the *Glentanner*. After arrival they were transhipped to Dunedin in the *Kate Kearney*. He built a house in Forth Street, Dunedin where he spent forty-five years. John worked as a carpenter. He was a member of the Knox Church and interested in the Sunday School. He was elected into the Dunedin City Council in 1874 and was re-elected in 1876.[124] Mrs Grant died before her husband, who passed away in 1901 of heart trouble. They left a son and daughter, nine grandchildren, and four great grandchildren.[125]

Hardesty

Benjamin Hardesty arrived in New Zealand on the *Glentanner* in 1857 with his daughter Elizabeth aged 27 and what appears to be his son Joseph aged 6. A boy named Joseph Hurdsley aged 8 died on board the *Glentanner*. This is likely to be Joseph Hardesty as there was no family named Hurdsley on board, unless they were unlisted, and a search of New Zealand records brings up no Hurdsley name. Benjamin lived at 161 Peterborough Street, Christchurch at one stage[126] and died in 1876 aged 82.[127] Elizabeth died in 1897 and was buried at Barbadoes Street Cemetery, Christchurch.[128] There was also a Mary Hardesty in the records, daughter of Benjamin, who never married and died in Belfast in 1890 aged 59 years.[86]

Hodgson

John and Elizabeth Hodgson were 58 and 59 when they came out to New Zealand, bringing five children with them. John Hodgson died in 1880 aged 82. He was residing in the Heathcote Valley at the time of his death. Elizabeth died in 1871 aged 75. Their daughter, Sophia, married Robert Gilkes in 1863.[86]

Holmes

George and Amelia Holmes came to New Zealand on the *Glentanner* with two children, Harriet and Frederick. Amelia died in 1885 aged 71 and was a widow, living in Sockburn at the time of her death. Frederick also lived in Sockburn.[129]

Horman

Carson Henry Horman (sometimes spelt Carston Hormann) was born in Germany, where he was brought up with farming. He came to New Zealand on the *Glentanner* in 1857 and settled in Southland. In 1859 he became the first settler of the Waikiwi district, where he bought 228 acres of heavy bush land. Carson was a member of the Waikiwi school committee. Carson married Christina Dorothea Gohl in 1859 and they had a family of ten sons and three daughters, of which two daughters died young.[130] Christina died in 1895 and Carson in 1904.[89]

Hymers

Barbara Hymers née Oliver, was born in Oldiebea, Caithness, Scotland in 1834. She was apparently on board the *Glentanner*. She married Andrew Hymers in 1854 in Halkirk, Caithness, Scotland. Andrew was likely on the *Glentanner* as well. Barbara's six month old baby, Jane Hymers, tragically died on board the ship. She had a twin brother on board named James Oliver Hymers who survived.[131] Barbara herself died on 12 October 1857 at Christchurch Hospital aged 22, only 9 days after arrival.[86] Andrew Hymers remarried a lady named Margaret and they had a daughter Helen in 1862. James Oliver Hymers lived until his late 70s, dying in 1934.[89]

Ivory

Aquila Ivory was born in Norwich, England, in 1830 and came to New Zealand on the *Glentanner* in 1857 with his wife. He settled in Rangiora as his brother, William, was already there. He helped to build some of the first roads in the district. He then became a grain buyer and shipper. He was a member of the Rangiora Borough Council and was Mayor of Rangiora twice. He married Miss Didcock in England, who died in 1898 in New Zealand.[132] At the time of her marriage she as in service to Lady Jane Bouverie, who was bridesmaid to Queen Victoria. She bravely faced the difficulties of the early settlers' life. She left a family of three behind.[133] Aquila died in 1908 and was buried in Rangiora.

Aquila was related to the Doggett family who was also on board the *Glentanner* as well as the Stapleforth and Jennings families who came on other ships. They all set up the first Baptist church in Canterbury, called "Little Bethel."[134] Ivory Street in Rangiora, was named after the Ivory family, which included Aquila's brother William.

Johnston

Elizabeth Johnston was born in Aberdeenshire and travelled to New Zealand on the *Glentanner* with her family. In 1868, she married William Johnston who was also born in Aberdeenshire, Scotland. He had studied farming in Scotland before travelling to New Zealand on the *Mystery*. William farmed at Yaldhurst on *Fernleigh Farm*. He had a large threshing business with help from his sons. Their surviving family consisted of five sons and two daughters.[135]

Mr. & Mrs. Johnston

Maber

Susanna and John Maber were from Guernsey. They travelled to New Zealand on the *Glentanner* in 1857. After arrival they had at least nine children, including 3 boys and 6 girls.[89] John was a farmer in the Kaiapoi Island area. Susanna died in 1910 aged 77 and was residing in Kaiapoi.

Marshall

A carpenter named Robert Marshall was in the single men's quarters on the *Glentanner*. There is a marriage for Robert Marshall, joiner, to Mary Anne Goodwin (a minor) on 1 March 1860 at St Michael's Christchurch. This is likely to be the correct Robert Marshall from the ship as he has the same occupation and age.[86] This couple had at least five children.[89]

McLennan

Murdo and Abigail McLennan were from Scotland. They came to New Zealand on the *Glentanner* with their four children. They moved from Canterbury to Otago in 1868. Abigail McLennan died at King Street, Dunedin in 1899, at the age of 75 years.[136]

McRae

George McRae was born in Ross-shire, Scotland in 1838 and learnt farming at a young age. He travelled to New Zealand on the *Glentanner*.

George was head shepherd at the Mesopotamia estate for 13 years, before buying a sheep run on the Rangitata. He then moved to Waipawa Downs and then bought Braemore Estate in the Cheviot district. He was chairman of the Cheviot County Council, and member of the Hurunui Rabbit Board and the local School Committee. George sold Braemore in 1900 and bought the Barford Estate of 53,760 acres on the north side of the Hinds River. He owned this estate until 1902. He then bought Ringwood, where he built a residence. He retired from farming.

Mr. McRae was one of thirty *Glentanner* passengers who met in Christchurch on the 3 October 1897, to celebrate the fortieth anniversary of their landing in New Zealand. In May 1903, he left New Zealand to pay a visit to the "Old Country."[137]

He had a seizure and ended up bed-ridden before his death in 1911.

He was known as a "sterling and unassuming gentleman" and was greatly missed in the community after his death.[138]

Milner

William James Milner was born in Yorkshire, England in 1836 and arrived in New Zealand on the *Glentanner*. William settled at Woodend and started farming there in 1858. In 1862, he moved to Amberley and farmed there for many years. He was very interested in ploughing matches and systematic practical farming. He studiednatural history and knew a lot about English birds. He was married in 1859 to Mary Mounsey and they had five sons and two daughters.[139] Mary died in 1910 and William in 1915.[140]

Oliver

William Oliver was born in Kent, England and educated in London. He married Emily Wagstaff in 1855 and they emigrated to New Zealand on the *Glentanner* two years later. On the voyage Emily gave birth to a son, but tragically he died shortly after birth. They ended up having one son and three daughters once in New Zealand. William and Emily settled at Hororata, and lived there for at least thirty-five years.[141] William first bought land of about 431 acres in 1860 which he called *Springhead* and had to put in a lot of hard work to get rid of the tussock, flax, toi-toi and raupo before it could be farmed. William carted wool to Christchurch in 1861, when there were no roads and only a few cuttings as a means of entering and coming out of the rivers and gullies. He did this until the advent of the traction engine. William was the first to cross the Wilberforce River with a team of horses. Things were expensive when he first arrived in New

Mr & Mrs W. Oliver

Zealand. For example he had to pay £75 a head for horses. He was a member of the local school committee, racing club and sports committee. Emily died in 1896.[142]

Oram

Charles Oram was born in Midsomer Norton, Somersetshire, England in 1834. He trained as a bootmaker and left on the *Glentanner* in 1857 for New Zealand. He worked as a bootmaker for six months and then moved to the Maori Bush near Kaiapoi, where he became a bush-sawyer. He tried his hand at the gold rush before settling in Kaiapoi and becoming a bootmaker again. In 1864 he built the Pier Hotel, which he ran for twelve years. He encouraged Cobb and Co. to run a coach between Christchurch, Rangiora and the Hurunui until the railway came.

Mr. C. Oram

With his brother H. H. Oram, Charles opened several hotels in Christchurch including "The Royal." He entered a partnership and became a merchant for a few years. He was a member of the Kaiapoi Borough Council and Waimakariri Harbour Board. He was one of the original promoters and directors of the woollen factory at Kaiapoi. He was president of the Cure Boating Club and member of the Kaiapoi fire police. He was also a Freemason and helped establish the Oddfellowship in Kaiapoi. Charles married Emma Jane Treleaven in 1867.[89] He died in 1900 in Kaiapoi, leaving a wife, seven sons and three daughters.[143] Edwin Parnham and William Bush (*Glentanner* shipmates) were pallbearers at his funeral.[144]

Paddy

Henry Paddy married Eliza Worsfold in 1862. They had at least three children, Henry, Frederick and Alice. They lived at Southbridge,[145] and Henry retired from business in the area in 1882.[146] Eliza died on 1 February 1891 and was residing at 27 Walker Street, Christchurch. She was in her 61st year.[147] Henry died on 19 February 1893 aged 58 years.[148]

Parnham

Edwin Parnham was born in Flintham, Nottinghamshire, England in 1835. His father was John Parnham who travelled to Lyttelton in 1858 on the *Indiana,* and died in Kaiapoi in Feb 1865. Edwin came out to New Zealand on the *Glentanner* in 1857. His first job was hand sawing at Kaiapoi native bush, but he suffered great loss due to the large fire of October 1859 that reduced thousands of feet of sawn timber and trees to ashes. He tried the Otago gold fields and was at Gabriel's Gully rush. He then returned to Kaiapoi and did butchery with his brother-in-law, Mr. W. H. Mein. He then

Mr E. Parnham

had his own business, which he handed over to his sons in 1891 so he could concentrate on farming. He had land at Kaiapoi Island and Sefton. He was a borough councillor and Mayor of Kaiapoi in 1883. He was a member of the Waimakariri Harbour Board when the Board first tried to dredge the river. He was a member of the School Committee and chairman of the Farmers' Club. He exhibited at the first Northern A. and P. Show in 1866. Edwin was one of the provisional directors on the prospectus of the Kaiapoi Woollen Manufacturing Company which was issued on 1 October 1880. He retained a seat on the Board for thirty years. He served in many other organisations and societies. He loved cricket and then became a bowler and had an excellent private green. He supported the Kaiapoi brass band and was part of the Oddfellows. In 1863, he married Mary Coe who died in 1899. Edwin married a second time to Miss Robb. When Edwin died in his 77th year in 1911, he left a widow and six sons.[149]

Pinner

Charlotte Pinner arrived in New Zealand in 1857 on the *Glentanner*. She was brought out by G. Scarborough, her future husband, along with the Oliver family.[70] She married George Thomas Scarborough[89], sawyer, in 1858 with fellow *Glentanner* passengers

Henry and Mary Ann Wagstaff as witnesses.[86] George became a publican at Bruce's Hotel, Akaroa in 1862.[150] George died at his residence in Akaroa in 1878, aged 49,[151] and was buried in the Church of England Cemetery in Akaroa.[152] Charlotte died in 1881 aged 54.[86]

Potts

James Potts was born in 1834 in Christ Church, Spitalfields, Middlesex, England to John and Elizabeth Potts (née Thompson). James arrived at Lyttelton on the ship *Glentanner* in 1857, listed as a basketmaker from London, aged 23. Even though it was a difficult journey out, this didn't stop James trying to sponsor his future wife, Sarah Winfield Brown to sail out on the *Gananoque* in 1860. In the end he didn't have to sponsor her as she became matron on the ship – her job being to keep the single women away from the single men and vice versa! Being matron meant she got free passage out. They married a month after Sarah arrived in New Zealand. James's occupation was labourer at the time.

On 18 August 1867, when his daughter was baptised, he was named as a Foreman of Government Works. James and Sarah had two stillbirths and two children, but both died as babies.

James became a Civil Engineer in New Zealand and was surveyor to the Waimakariri Board of Works. How he rose to such a position after being a humble basketmaker is unknown. They lived in a cottage 16 miles from town somewhere near Halkett on what is now the Old West Coast Road. Even though James had no children he was a member of the Halkett School Committee. He was also chairman of the Halkett Church Committee in April 1873. James was churchwarden in May 1875, when an addition was made to the Courtenay Church and a spire was added. The Bishop consecrated the Church.

James Potts was chairman of the Halkett School Committee at the time of his death on 25 October 1879 at his home in Courtenay, aged a young 44. Sarah remarried to Karl Philipp Meng and gained three step daughters, who said that the stories of mean step-mothers weren't always true.[153]

Pringle

John and Agnes Pringle (née Oliver) and William and Isabella Pringle (née Oliver) where brothers and sisters who married each other. They all came out to New Zealand on the *Glentanner* from Scotland. Francis Pringle (another brother) also came out. This family are not on the original passenger list but a child, James Pringle aged 16 months, died on board the ship and was listed in the newspapers. James was the son of William and Isabella.[154]

John and Agnes Pringle had twelve children in New Zealand,[89] and at one stage were living in Livingstone, North Otago. Their son John Pringle died in an accident on 29 November 1898.[155]

The Oliver sisters were not related to William and Emily Oliver who were also on board the ship and were from Kent, but were related to Barbara Hymers (née Oliver).

Ramscar

George and Ann Mary Ramscar were from Lincolnshire, England. George was a bootmaker in Christchurch. He had ten years in Christchurch before dying in 1867, aged 58 years.[89] Ann died in 1883 aged 82 and was residing in Chester Street East, Christchurch at the time of her death. They are both buried in Barbadoes Street Cemetery, Christchurch.[86]

Robinson

Ward Robinson came to New Zealand on the *Glentanner* in 1857. He became an early settler of Springfield, where he took up farming. He was involved with the church and was churchwarden at Springfield for many years. Ward had an honourable and generous character, which was held in high esteem by members of the community. He passed away in 1898, aged 80 years.[156] Ward was the oldest *Glentanner* passenger who attended the 40th anniversary of the ship's arrival. He died not long after. The youngest of the passengers at that celebration, Mrs Legge, also died just after the function.[157]

Rogers

James Rogers arrived in New Zealand on the *Glentanner* in 1857 and started worked for some time for the Deans family. He helped convert the wilderness at Riccarton into pastoral land. He saw Christchurch turn from a small village into a prosperous city. James was one of the first settlers to buy land in Templeton, where he farmed for over 30 years. He didn't take part in public life much but was one of the founders of the Anglican Church in Templeton and was churchwarden for some years. James retired to Christchurch. Old residents came a long way to pay their respects to him when he died in 1914.[158]

Rollo

James and Janet Rollo came out with the Boag family to New Zealand on the *Glentanner*. James was listed as a son-in-law to the Boag family. They had at least five children as follows: William, born 1863; Janet, born 1865; Ann, born 1866; Mary Alexandra, born 1869; James John Arklie, born 1873.[89]

Rossiter

Maria Rossiter travelled in the single women's quarters on the *Glentanner*, arriving in New Zealand on 3 October 1857. She had married Abraham Palmer in New Zealand before the end of 1857.[89]

Rutland

Walter George Rutland travelled to New Zealand on the *Glentanner*. He was a carpenter by trade and ended up settling in Temuka.[159] He went bankrupt in 1879 and had to sell his 4 and a half acre property including well built dwelling and out-buildings as well as a garden full of the best fruit trees. His house was in a prime part of Temuka.[160] He married Eleanor Langbridge in 1862 and they had at least five children.[89] Walter died in 1927 aged 85.[89]

Walter's older brother, Edwin Rutland, moved to Southland in 1863. He was a collector of newspapers and had a copy of the 1857 newspaper with the *Glentanner* journey summary and passenger list.[161] In 1901, Edwin presented to Southland Hospital, a bound volume of newspapers, one from every year dating from 1863 to 1901. He was a bookbinder by trade. He was sexton of St John's Church, Invercargill from 1865–1871 and wrote a diary while in the position.[162]

Selfe

Alexander Selfe and his wife, Martha, were on the *Glentanner* in 1857. They never had any children. Alexander worked as a carpenter and builder in Christchurch. He was an alcoholic and ended up drowned in the Avon River, between the Madras Street bridge and the Brick's Wharf in January 1866. The night before his death he told Inspector Pender, "I have been on the "lush" about a week ago but I have not taken anything to drink lately." Alexander appeared to be under the influence of delirium tremens. He was found the next day, face down in the river, wearing only a Crimean shirt and a flannel under-waistcoat.[163] Martha was left a widow, but remarried in 1868 to Thomas George Moule.[89] She died in 1891 aged 71 years.[89]

Snelling

Jane Snelling arrived on the *Glentanner* in 1857, aged 43, and soon afterwards married Robert Taylor, a builder aged 45, on 8 February 1858 at Wesleyan Chapel, Lyttelton.[86] Robert was a widower and Jane a spinster. It appears that they probably had no children.[89]

Spring

Walter Spring was born in London in 1838 and arrived on the *Glentanner* in 1857. His first job in Canterbury was as a surveyor's assistant and he helped to lay out the roads in and around Christchurch. He then caught "gold fever" and went to Bendigo and other big gold rushes in Australia. He also went to the Gabriel's Gully gold rush in Otago. He managed the Leeston Hotel in 1867 and subsequently became owner of the property, which he developed into a fine country hotel. He retired to Christchurch in 1892. He was a sportsman and raced a number of good horses in New Zealand, under the turf name of W. Russell. He owned the horses Irish King, The Idler, Silver Queen, Bay King, Carronade and Magpie. Walter was into cycle racing and built a track at Leeston.

He married twice and left a family of grown-up sons and daughters from both marriages. He was in an "unostentatious way, a benevolent man, and respected by those who knew his sterling qualities."[164]

Stubbs

Abraham Stubbs was a passenger on the *Glentanner* in 1857. He became a farmer in the Canterbury area. He went missing in 1862 after drinking at a hotel, and there was a long article entitled "Disappearance of Abraham Stubbs. Discovery of the Body. Suspicion of Foul Play." Abraham was found face down in the Avon River. A man named John Groves was under suspicion of murdering Abraham. It seems that Groves went to seek his fortune on the goldfields and left his wife behind. She led a life of debauchery while he was away and Abraham was involved! Groves didn't like Abraham Stubbs one bit.[165] After many witnesses being questioned and the coroner's report finding Abraham and died from drowning, the court could not prosecute Groves as there wasn't enough evidence. However, they thought it highly likely he was involved. He had been very jumpy when Abraham's body had been found and had a strong motive for murder.[166]

Swale

William S. Swale travelled to New Zealand on the *Glentanner*, leaving his wife Elizabeth and three children, William, Mary and Sarah behind. Elizabeth and the children arrived a year later on the *Zealandia*. William was a gardener, who wrote numerous letters to the editor on the subject of gardening in Canterbury.[167] They are an amazing record of early gardening. He ran the Avonside Botanical and Horticultural Gardens, a 2 ¾ acre block where he sold plants and trees. He was also a reporter, writing for the Gardener's Chronicle (an English periodical), and his work is now quite famous. William even corresponded with Charles Darwin, who honoured him by quoting him in lectures. William had no nose and often people couldn't understand him very well. One day he got into a verbal fight with Henry John Tancred, who had a speech impediment. No one could understand what either of them was saying! William died in 1875, aged 59, and his son, William, only three years later.[168] His eldest daughter, Mary Eliza Potter Swale, got married in 1878 in Avonside, Christchurch.[169] Elizabeth died in 1903.[170]

Thomas

Richard Dunn Thomas was born in England in 1838. After arriving on the *Glentanner,* he spent many years farming and held the Benmore Station, near Porter's Pass. He then studied law with Mr. T. I. Joynt, and became a barrister and solicitor in 1871. He eventually had his own practice. He was chairman of the Hospital Board and president of the Canterbury Rowing Club and the Canterbury Society of Arts. He became Master of the St Augustine Lodge in 1874 and was re-elected to the position in 1882. He was District Grand Master of the Canterbury E. C. (Masonic Order). He died very suddenly in 1904 just after addressing the Art Society. He had been playing bowls the day before his death.[171]

Wagstaff

Henry and Mary Ann Wagstaff (née Whiley) and six children (including Emily Oliver, née Wagstaff, and her husband) came to New Zealand on the *Glentanner* in 1857. Henry was recorded as being a wheelwright. Another Henry Wagstaff (possibly a son) married Sarah Ann Taylor. He was a coach builder and worked at the Trollaway Works.[172] There was a Charles Wagstaff, coach builder, who died in 1873, aged 39, whose next of kin was Henry and Mary Ann Wagstaff.[86] Mary Ann Wagstaff died in 1887 at the Oliver's house in Hororata (her daughter's house) aged 75 years old.[173]

Ward

William John Ward left London aged 18 on the *Glentanner*. He married Sarah Elizabeth Ann Swanston (née Cole) in 1884 and they had at least one son Arthur Stanley Ward born in 1887.[89] William, a farmer, died in Christchurch in 1899 aged 59 years old.[174]

Wearing

Selina Wearing and her two children were passengers on the *Glentanner* in 1857. She was meeting her husband in the colony.

His name was George Herbert Wearing. The family lived in Kaiapoi. George testified at the inquest of his son-in-law who committed suicide in 1886.[175] George died in 1893 aged 70.[176] Selina died in 1911 aged 84.[177]

Wyatt

Alfred Ambrose Wyatt was only 14 when he left his home in Bristol and travelled to New Zealand on the *Glentanner*. He married Charlotte Loader in 1877. They had a family of at least five girls and three boys.[89] He died in 1895, aged 50, in Timaru of "Accidental death caused by haemorrhage on the brain." He was riding a dray and fell off straight on his face. He was not too bad and went home, but tragically died that afternoon.[178]

Second Voyage to New Zealand
(24 February 1861 – 8 June 1861)

Second Voyage to New Zealand 1861

The *Glentanner* left the Downs (an area of sea in the North Sea) on 24 February 1861 and arrived in Lyttelton, New Zealand on 8 June 1861 with Captain Wilson at the helm and 24 cabin passengers.[179] There were no government-assisted emigrants on board. The journey took 104 days. The ship left the Downs at the same time as the ship *Mersey* (for Auckland) and the Swedish brig *Gylfe* (also for Lyttelton). The *Glentanner* passed the *Gylfe* the next day.

On 7 March, the passengers sent letters on board the barque *Eliza*, which was heading for England. There would have been much excitement. Often passengers ran around in a frenzy, looking for paper and pens to scrawl a quick message before the sack of letters was taken over to the homeward bound ship. They may have only written a few lines, but it reassured the family and friends back at home.

The *Glentanner* passed Madeira on 12 March 1861 and crossed the line (equator) on 28 March.

It took almost another month for the ship to reach the meridian of the Cape on 25 April. Up until this time they enjoyed lovely fine weather, but from 14 to 16 May they struck a heavy gale from the west. One can imagine the passengers battened down inside the ship so that the crew could do their job on board.

On 20 May 1861, they passed the meridian of Tasmania and a few days later, on 4 June, they sighted Stewart Island. They endured heavy weather all the way from the Cape to Lyttelton.

The newspapers commented on the previous refitting of a new mainmast and spars at Pigeon Bay, and how they were still in place, having done the job very well. They were called "remarkably good sticks."

The *Glentanner* had different owners, Messrs. Wilson of Plymouth, England.[7]

The *Gylfe* ended up arriving on 14 July 1861, over a month behind *Glentanner*. The newspapers noted the delay.[180] The following report showed that the *Glentanner* narrowly missed being stuck in the channel for weeks on end:

"The Swedish brig *Gylfe,* Captain Prahn, arrived in harbour on Sunday afternoon, after a long passage of 140 days from London. She sailed from the Downs on the 24th of February, and was detained three weeks in the Channel by contrary winds; crossed the line on the 2nd of April, and experienced continued bad weather with hurricanes to the Cape. Made her easting principally in the high latitude of 39, meeting with very changeable weather; sighted the Snares, and arrived here on the 14th instant. Reports the loss of two of her crew from natural causes."[181]

The *Glentanner* departed for Callao on 4 August 1861, in ballast and, soon after, met her watery grave off the coast of Brazil.[182]

Glentanner Cargo 1861

A newspaper report noted that some of the *Glentanner* cargo was very precious to the colony: "The *Glentanner* brings, as an important part of her cargo for this port, 31 Spanish sheep consigned to Messrs. Miles and Co, for Mr. Geo. Rich, and 5 Hampshire Downs rams. The former consist of 10 pure Spanish merino ewes, and 10 others of the same blood crossed with one-third French; these 20 ewes have 11 lambs, which complete the number. Five lambs were lost on the way out; the remainder are in as good condition as when put on board. These fine sheep are from Mr. Rich's English flocks and, like all that gentleman's importations, are quite a spectacle for a connoisseur in sheep." [183]

A Ship of Wool and Sheep

The name *Glentanner* was used for a famous sheep station in the Mackenzie Country and it delivered wool back to England in 1858. In 1861, it brought merino and other sheep to New Zealand. We can therefore state that the *Glentanner* had a great impact on early sheep farming and wool exports in New Zealand.

Map of the Journey of the *Glentanner* 1861

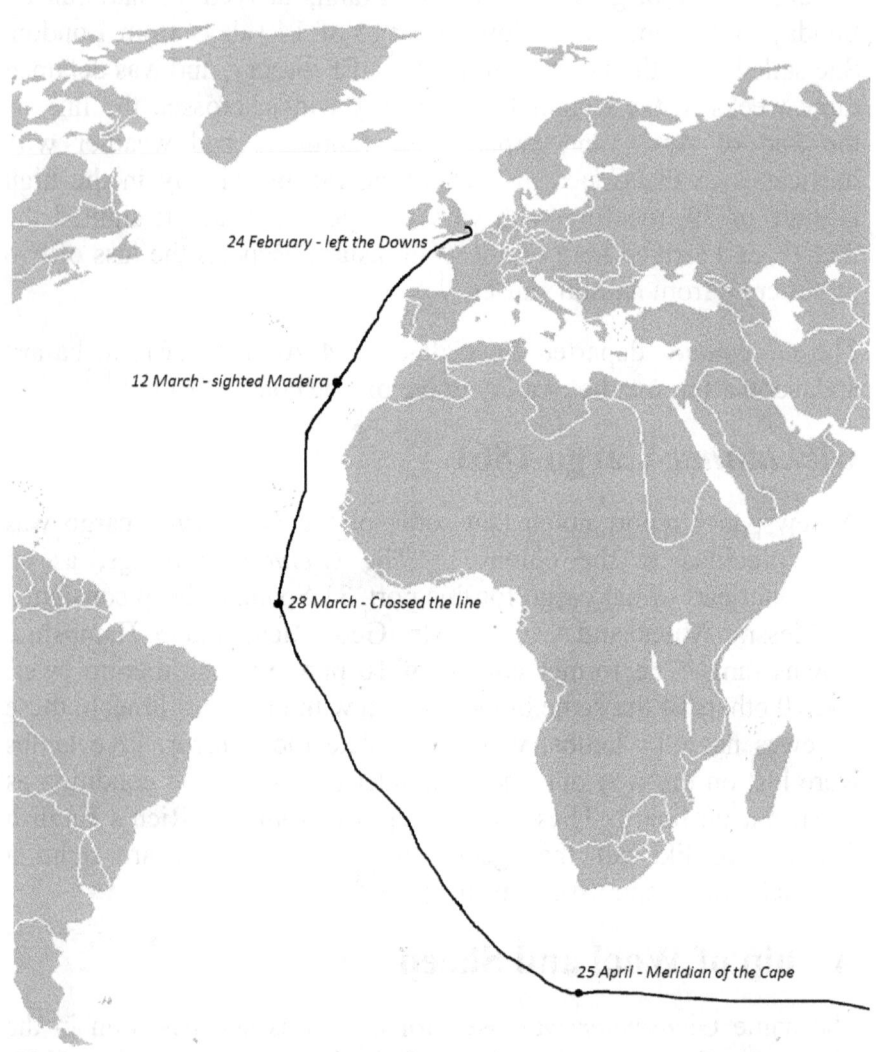

(24 February 1861 – 8 June 1861)

Second Voyage to New Zealand

24 February 1851 – 9 June 1851

Passengers on the 1861 Voyage

Passengers on the 1861 Voyage

Curry

In the early 1850s, Edward Curry was asked by a Mr Longden to purchase and send sections of a steamer out to New Zealand. The steamer was called *Avon* by Miss Cholmondeley, daughter of Archdeacon Cholmondeley of Opawa, Christchurch. The *Avon* was used for carrying stores for the troops during the Maori war. Edward came to New Zealand on board the *Glentanner* in 1861 after being convinced to emigrate by a man he went to school with, Mr. W. J. W. Hamilton, collector of customs and Mr Joseph Longden. His wife was on board with him. Once Edward arrived, he lived at Mount Torlesse Station for six years, which he bought and then sold to Mr Karslake and Mr Anson. He then moved to Waireka station and also managed Bangor and Glendore Station. He sold Waireka station. He died at the age of 81 in 1902.[184]

Passenger Lists

The following lists have been transcribed directly from the passenger lists of steerage passengers, with cabin passengers taken from newspaper articles. Corrections were made after research was done on the passengers.

Passengers 1857

Crew

Surname	Given Name	Age	Location	Occupation/Notes
Bruce	Benjamin			Captain
Ellis	Thomas			Surgeon *(came with three daughters, see below)*
Silva	Augustus			Sailor **Died on voyage**

Chief Cabin

Surname	Given Name	Age	Location	Occupation/Notes
Ellis	Miss			
Ellis	Miss			
Ellis	Miss			
Miles	H.			
Oalton	R.			*(For Otago)*
Thomas	R. D.			
Turnbull	J.			
Colborne-Veel [Veil]	Mr. J. V. [J. C]			
Colborne-Veel [Veil]	Mrs			
Zouch	T. A.			

Second Cabin

Surname	Given Name	Age	Location	Occupation/Notes
Brugh [Burgh]	S. (Sheddan)			*(For Otago)*
Groves	J.			

Groves	Mary				
Henderson	J.				*(For Otago)*
Milner	J.				
Patner	J. B.				
Wearing	Selina	24		London	*(Married) Husband in Colony*
Wearing	George	7			
Wearing	Blanche	2			

Government Immigrants

Married Couples

Surname	Given Name	Age	Location	Occupation/ Notes
Boag	William	50	Scotland	Farm Servant
	Jane	49		Farm Servant
Rollo	Janet	21		Farm Servant - *Came with Boag. Wife of James Rollo.*
Boag	Ann	19	Scotland	Farm Servant
	John	16	Scotland	Farm Servant
	Peter	10		*Boy at School*
Rollo	James	25	Scotland	Labourer - *Son In Law of Boag*
Bradwell	Caroline	35	Sheffield	*Husband a printer in the Colony*
	Albert	10		
	Caroline	7		
Brooks	Henry	30	London	Labourer
	Elizabeth	28		
	Henry	4		
	John	2		
	Joseph	11 mths		
Clement	Shadrack	26	Somersetshire	Agricultural Labourer
	Elizabeth	28		

	William Henry	6		
	Elizabeth Ann	4		
	Edward Charles	2		
Craythorne	William	39	Leicestershire	Farm Labourer
	Mary	39		
	Mary Ann	18		Servant
	Fanny	14		Servant
	Charles	11		Servant
	Emma	7		
Day	Daniel	34	Bristol	Bricklayer
	Mary	43		
	Robert	10		
	Eliza	8		
Doggett	William	36	Suffolk	Labourer
	Matilda	41		
	Hannah	11		
	Rebecca	8		
	Maria	5		
	John	4		
	Lucy	1		
East	Sarah	37	Oxfordshire	Upholsterer & Milliner *(Widow)*
	Harry	17		Upholsterer
	Frank W.	13		
	Alfred E. P.	10		
	Herbert E.	8		
Fielder (Feilder in newspaper)	Henry	31	London	Carpenter
	Emma	23		
	Sarah Ann	10		
	Henry	8		
	Infant (John in newspaper)	10 mths		

Passenger Lists

Galletly (Gallitly in newspaper)	Peter	27	Perthshire	Ploughman
	Marjory	24		
	John	3		
	Infant	7 mths		
Hardesty (Hardisty in newspaper)	Benjamin	60	Norfolk	Labourer
	Elizabeth	27		Servant *(Daughter of above)*
	Joseph	6		
Hodgson	John	58	London	Bootmaker
	Elizabeth	59		
	Mary	26		
	Jane	24		
	Sophia	18		
	Henry	12		
Hodgson	John	23	London	Carpenter
	Sophia	26		
Holmes	George	45	Allington, Wiltshire	Agricultural Labourer
	Amelia	44		
	Harriet	16		
	Frederick	12		
Ivory	Aquila	28	London	Gardener
	Ann	28		
	Louisa	3		
	William (Aquila in newspaper)	11 mths		**Died on voyage**
Johnston	John	40	Scotland	Smith & Implement Maker
	Elizabeth M.	35		
	Alexander	14		
	William	12		

Passenger Lists

	Elizabeth	10		
	Helen	9		
	John	6		
	James Moir	4		
	Peter Martin	2		
Maber	John	23	Guernsey	Labourer
	Susanna	25	Guernsey	Domestic Servant *(note on pass. list "formerly Emma Glanville")*
McLennan	Murdo	41	Scotland	Shepherd
	Abigail	29		
	Mary	8		
	John	6		
	Kenneth	3		
	Alexander	2		
McLeod	Alexander	23	Scotland	Shepherd
	Mary	20		
Oliver	William	24	London	Labourer
	Emily	21		
	Son			***Born on board Died shortly after birth***
Ramscar	George	45	London	Bootmaker
	Ann Mary	47		
Robinson	Ward	35	Lincolnshire	Gardener
	Mary	33		
	Anna	9		
	Louisa J.	8		
	Harriet	6		
	Elizabeth	5		
	Ward	3		
	George	18 mths		***Died on voyage***
	Son			***Born on board***

Selfe	Alexander	34	England	Carpenter
	Martha	?		
Wagstaff	Henry	47	London	Carpenter
	Mary Ann	43		
	Mary Ann	18		Domestic Servant
	Charlotte	15		
	Matilda	12		
	Caroline	10		
	Jessie	7		
Gredus	Selina	19		Domestic Servant - *Came with Wagstaff*

Single Men

Surname	*Given Name*	*Age*	*Location*	*Occupation/ Notes*
Barton	Henry	20	London	Carpenter
Bush	William	23	Essex	Carpenter
Chappell	Edwin	16	London	Butcher
Dawson	Thomas	23	Macclesfield	Labourer
Dobbs	Joseph Manning	10	Ireland	
Elliott	Robert	21	Nottingham	Blacksmith
Evans	William	22	London	Porter & Waiter
Forbes	William	16	Scotland	Domestic Servant
Galletly	David	24	Scotland	Shepherd
Johnston	Alexander	44	Scotland	Smith & Implement Maker
Marshall	Robert	24	Nottinghamshire	Carpenter
McRae	George	20	Scotland	Shepherd
Merrin	James	24	Nottinghamshire	Labourer
Oram	Matthew Henry	25	London	Bootmaker
Oram	Charles	23	London	Bootmaker
Paddy	Henry	22	London	Agricultural Labourer &

					Baker
Parnham	Edwin	22	Nottinghamshire		Joiner
Potts	James	23	London		Basket Maker
Rogers	James	22	Nottinghamshire		Farm Labourer
Rutland	Walter George	16	London and Taplow Berks		Carpenter
Rutland	Edwin	18	Berkshire		Carpenter
Stubbs	Abraham	30	Cheshire		Labourer
Swale	William	39	Manchester		Gardener
Taylor	John	25	Hampshire		Labourer
Ward	William John	18	London		Carpenter
Williams	Thomas	14	Bedfordshire		Servant Boy
Wyatt	Alfred Ambrose	14	Bristol		Labourer

Single Women

Surname	*Given Name*	*Age*	*Location*	*Occupation/ Notes*
Allen	Martha	14	London	Servant
Didcock	Esther	24	Bucks	Domestic Servant
Dobbs	Rebecca M.	45	Ireland	Nurse *(Widow)*
Pinner (Primer in newspaper)	Charlotte	26	London	Servant *(came with Oliver)*
Rossiter	Maria	24	Somersetshire	Servant
Snelling	Jane	43	Oxfordshire	Servant
Topp	Mary	49	Cambridgeshire	Servant
Williams	Mary	38	Bedfordshire	Servant

Confirmed passengers, not on original passenger list

Surname	*Given Name*	*Age*	*Location*	*Occupation/ Notes*
Dark	Edward			*Not in paper or passenger list*[67]
Dark	Cornelius			
East	Frederick Charles			*On the Glentanner according to his obituary.*[111]

Grant	John				*(for Otago) Not on original passenger list.*[124]
Grant	Mrs				
Grant	Son				
Grant	Daughter				
Harrison	Edward	?	?		*Listed in newspaper*
Hymers	Andrew				*Not on original list*[131]
Hymers	Barbara				*Died just after voyage, 1857*
Hymers	Jane	6 mths			**Died on voyage**
Hymers	James Oliver	6 mths			*Twin to Jane*
Hurdsley (maybe Hardesty?)	Joseph	8			**Died on voyage**
Pringle	John				*Not on original list*[131]
Pringle	Agnes				
Pringle	William				
Pringle	Isabella				
Pringle	Jane	7			
Pringle	Helen	5			
Pringle	James	16 mths			**Died on voyage**
Pringle	Francis				*Brother to John and William*[185]
Unconfirmed passengers (not proven)					
Wheeler	Jane				*Two Wheelers listed with the Holmes family as gone out in the Glentanner, but not on the main passenger list.*[70]
Wheeler	Sarah				

Passenger Lists

Passengers 1861

Crew

Surname	Given Name	Age	Location	Occupation/Notes
Wilson	H.			Captain

Chief Cabin

Surname	Given Name	Age	Location	Occupation/Notes
Curry	Mr. Edward			
Curry	Mrs.			
Campbell	Mr.			
Radford	Mr.			
Smith	Mr.			
Caser	Mr.			
Jones	Mr.			
Thistlewaite (Thistlewayte)	Mr.			

Second Cabin

Surname	Given Name	Age	Location	Occupation/Notes
Neeve	Mr.			
Neeve	Mrs.			
Neeve	Seven children			
Scott	Mr.			
Scott	Mrs.			
Gaynor	Mr.			
Brown	Mr.			
Craighead	Mr.			
Lake	Mr.			
Neilson	Mr.			

References

1. Aberdeen Maritime Museum, A. C. C. Aberdeen Ships | Alexander Hall & Sons Ltd. at <http://www.aberdeenships.com/sb_alexander_hall.asp>
2. Lloyd's Register of Shipping. *Books Boxes Boats* at <http://www.maritimearchives.co.uk/lloyds-register.html>
3. What is a Clipper Ship? | Marine Insight. at <http://www.marineinsight.com/marine/life-at-sea/maritime-history/what-is-a-clipper-ship-2/>
4. Aberdeen Maritime Museum, A. C. C. Aberdeen Ships | GLENTANAR. at <http://www.aberdeenships.com/single.asp?offset=1140&index=100044>
5. History and Geology of Glen Tanar - Aberdeenshire. at <http://www.glentanar.co.uk/history.html>
6. Shipping News. Court case. Benjamin Bruce. 13 July 1859. *Lyttelton Times* 4 (1859).
7. Heathcote River. Glentanner arrival 12 June 1861. *Lyttelton Times* 4 (1861).
8. Wikipedia contributors. Packet ship. *Wikipedia, the free encyclopedia* (2012). at <http://en.wikipedia.org/w/index.php?title=Packet_ship&oldid=481049374>
9. Wikipedia contributors. New Zealand Company. *Wikipedia, the free encyclopedia* (2012). at <http://en.wikipedia.org/w/index.php?title=New_Zealand_Company&oldid=491507428>
10. The Mersey clipper ship - Cossar.co.nz. at <http://www.cossar.co.nz/c-mersey.htm>
11. Taonga, N. Z. M. for C. and H. T. M. Settlement in the provinces: 1853 to 1870. at <http://www.teara.govt.nz/en/history-of-immigration/5>
12. Acland, J. B. A. Shipping papers 'Clontarf, A1': ships regulations and plan. University of Canterbury. Acland. (1855).
13. Shaw, Savill And Albion Company | NZETC. at <http://nzetc.victoria.ac.nz/tm/scholarly/tei-Bre01Whit-t1-body-d5.html>
14. Costs and Wages in Great Britain. at <http://www.rootsweb.ancestry.com/~irlcar2/wages.htm>
15. Purdy, F. On the Earnings of Agricultural Labourers in England and Wales, 1860. *Journal of the Statistical Society of London* **24**, 328–373 (1861).
16. Life at Sea: Museum Victoria. at <http://museumvictoria.com.au/discoverycentre/websites-mini/journeys-australia/1850s70s/life-at-sea/>
17. Diver, M. *The Voyages of the Clontarf*. (Dornie Publishing Company, 2011).
18. SYDNEY. 12 October 1843. *Launceston Advertiser* 3 (1843).
19. SHIPPING INTELLIGENCE. ARRIVED. 23 December 1843. *The Australian* 2 (1843).
20. Shipping intelligence, arrived. 13 January 1844. *The Australian* 2 (1844).
21. SHIPPING INTELLIGENCE. ARRIVED. NONE. SAILED. 20 February 1844. *The Australian* 2 (1844).
22. Advertising. Glentanner 22 January 1844. *The Sydney Morning Herald* 1 (1844).
23. Sydney News. SHIPPING INTELLIGENCE. (From the Sydney Morning Herald.) ARRIVALS. 23 June 1847. *The Maitland Mercury & Hunter River General Advertiser* 2 (1847).
24. SHIPPING INTELLIGENCE. ARRIVED. 19 June 1847. *The Australian* 2 (1847).
25. Shipping Intelligence. ARRIVALS. Glentanner. 19 June 1847. *Sydney Chronicle* 2 (1847).
26. DEPARTURES. The Glentanner. 28 July 1847. *Sydney Chronicle* 2 (1847).
27. Archway :: Item Full Description. Tenders for emigrant ships - List of tenders received in pursuance of the advertisement dated 4 May 1848 - 'Glentanner' (ship) - Rating A1 - 524 tons (old) - Owner JR Johnston. R17496836. at <http://www.archway.archives.govt.nz/ViewFullItem.do?code=17496836>
28. Shipping Intelligence. ARRIVED. 4 April 1850. *The Argus* 2 (1850).
29. HOBART TOWN. 10 April 1850. *The Sydney Morning Herald* 2 (1850).
30. Chinese in Guyana: Their Roots. at <http://www.rootsweb.ancestry.com/~guycigtr/>
31. Chinese in Guyana: Their Roots. at <http://www.rootsweb.ancestry.com/~guycigtr/>
32. Chinese in Guyana: Their Roots. at <http://www.rootsweb.ancestry.com/~guycigtr/>
33. MELBOURNE. ARRIVED. 30 September 1853. *Geelong Advertiser and Intelligencer* 2 (1853).
34. IMMIGRATION. 25 July 1853. *The Courier* 3 (1853).
35. VICTORIA. 18 July 1853. *The Sydney Morning Herald* 2 (1853).
36. SHIPPING INTELLIGENCE. GEELONG. ARRIVED. 9 May 1854. *Geelong Advertiser and*

Intelligencer 4 (1854).
37. THE GLENTANNER. 27 November 1855. *South Australian Register* 2 (1855).
38. SOUTH AUSTRALIA. [FROM OUR CORRESPONDENT.] 7 December 1855. *The Sydney Morning Herald* 3 (1855).
39. SHIPPING INTELLIGENCE. ARRIVED. 27 November 1855. *South Australian Register* 2 (1855).
40. VESSELS LOADING. Glentanner. 19 May 1859. *The Maitland Mercury & Hunter River General Advertiser* 3 (1859).
41. Local Intelligence. 9 July 1859. *The Moreton Bay Courier* 2 (1859).
42. Local Intelligence. RUMOUR OF THE GLENTANNER. 25 June 1859. *The Moreton Bay Courier* 2 (1859).
43. SHIPPING. ARRIVALS—AUGUST 31. Glentanner from Morton Bay to Sydney. 1 September 1859. *Empire* 4 (1859).
44. DEPARTURE.—SEPTEMBER 12. Glentanner. 13 September 1859. *The Sydney Morning Herald* 4 (1859).
45. Callao To Valparaiso. 10 January 1871. *North Otago Times* 2 (1871).
46. Heathcote River. How the Glentanner came to an end. 30 April 1862. *Lyttelton Times* 4 (1862).
47. The wreck of the Glentanner. 3 February 1862. *The Morning Chronicle (London)*
48. Archway :: Item Full Description. A. Willis Gunn to J.R. Godley - 'Glentanner' - 27/08/1857 (R22186416). at <http://www.archway.archives.govt.nz/ViewFullItem.do?code=22186416>
49. Archway :: Item Full Description. Blackford (Emigration) to Provincial Secretary - passages per Glentanner - 6/10/1857. R22186499. at <http://www.archway.archives.govt.nz/ViewFullItem.do?code=22186499>
50. Vivid Memory. Mrs Rebecca Bradley. 21 August 1936. *Auckland Star* 5 (1936).
51. Shipping News. Glentanner arrival and passenger and cargo lists. 7 October 1857. *Lyttelton Times* 4 (1857).
52. beam-ends - definition and meaning. *Wordnik.com* at <http://www.wordnik.com/words/beam-ends>
53. Glossary of nautical terms. *Wikipedia, the free encyclopedia* (2012). at <http://en.wikipedia.org/w/index.php?title=Glossary_of_nautical_terms&oldid=530505611>
54. The Glentanner | NZETC. at <http://nzetc.victoria.ac.nz/tm/scholarly/tei-Bre01Whit-t1-body-d284.html>
55. Cutty Sark. *Wikipedia, the free encyclopedia* (2013). at <http://en.wikipedia.org/w/index.php?title=Cutty_Sark&oldid=547705302>
56. Brockelbank, C. *Old Kaiapoi: a collection of memoirs*. (1941).
57. Correspondence. Benjamin Bruce, Letter to the Editor. 14 October 1857. *Lyttelton Times* 5 (1857).
58. Local Intelligence. Glentanner would have been total loss if mast hadn't snapped. 7 October 1857. *Lyttelton Times* 5 (1857).
59. Shipping News. Glentanner for Pigeon Bay. 4 November 1857. *Lyttelton Times* 4 (1857).
60. Election Of Superintendent. Glentanner to sit in port for two months. 4 November 1857. *Lyttelton Times* 4 (1857).
61. The Story of the Doggett Family. Rebecca Bradley. 9 November 1933. *North Canterbury Gazette*
62. Shipping News. Kate Kearney. 24 November 1857. *Colonist* 2 (1857).
63. Arrived. Kate Kearney 31 October 1857. *Otago Witness* 5 (1857).
64. The Lyttelton Times. Wednesday, October 17. Glentanner repairs. 17 October 1857. *Lyttelton Times* 5 (1857).
65. Local Intelligence. Glentanner refit complete. 2 January 1858. *Lyttelton Times* 5 (1858).
66. The Lyttelton Times. 2 January 1858. *Lyttelton Times* 5 (1858).
67. Sheepfarmers | NZETC. Glentanner Station. at <http://nzetc.victoria.ac.nz/tm/scholarly/tei-Cyc03Cycl-t1-body1-d6-d118-d2.html>
68. The Original Runholders by T. D. Burnett. 10 July 1925. *The Timaru Herald*
69. Sir John Cracroft Wilson. C.B., K.C.S.I | NZETC. at <http://nzetc.victoria.ac.nz/tm/scholarly/tei-Cyc03Cycl-t1-body1-d3-d6-d13.html>
70. View Images — FamilySearch.org - Glentanner Passenger list 1859. at <https://familysearch.org/pal:/MM9.3.1/TH-266-11691-146266-60?cc=1609792&wc=MMBG-R9B:1017701277>

71. Lyttelton Regatta. 6 January 1858. *Lyttelton Times* 5 (1858).
72. Shipping News. Glentanner for London with two passengers. 7 April 1858. *Lyttelton Times* 5 (1858).
73. Canterbury. Glentanner 'full as an egg' 24 April 1858. *Nelson Examiner and New Zealand Chronicle* 3 (1858).
74. Local Intelligence. Glentanner full of wool. 7 April 1858. *Lyttelton Times* 5 (1858).
75. Latest European, Foreign, And Indian, Intelligence. Glentanner arrives in London. 30 October 1858. *Wellington Independent* 3 (1858).
76. Local Intelligence. Glentanner set sail with cargo of wool. 10 April 1858. *Lyttelton Times* 4 (1858).
77. [BY ELECTRIC TELEGRAPH.] MELBOURNE. DEPARTURES. 21 May 1859. *The Sydney Morning Herald* 6 (1859).
78. Shipping News. Glentanner court case regarding crew wages. 31 December 1858. *Lyttelton Times* 4 (1858).
79. News Of The Day. Glentanner Reunion. 4 October 1897. *Press* 4 5 (1897).
80. News Of The Day. Shipmates reunion. 5 October 1897. *Press* 4 5 (1897).
81. Local And General. 40th reunion of the Glentanner. 5 October 1897. *Star* 3 (1897).
82. News Of The Day. Glentanner reunion. 13 November 1897. *Press* 7 (1897).
83. Personal Items. Glentanner Reunion. 4 December 1902. *Press* 5 (1902).
84. The Glentanner Jubiler. 5 October 1907. *Press* 7 (1907).
85. Reunion of Glentanner. 9 October 1907. *Canterbury Times* (1907).
86. *Christchurch Parish Records. Peterborough Central Library, Christchurch.*
87. Resident Magistrate's Court. Amelia Barton brothel owner. 28 March 1877. *Timaru Herald* 3 4 (1877).
88. TDC Cemetery Database. Amilia Barton burial. at <http://www.timaru.govt.nz/cemetery-database2.html>
89. Birth, Death and Marriage Historical Records. at <https://www.bdmhistoricalrecords.dia.govt.nz/home/>
90. Farmers | NZETC. Mr J. Boag. at <http://nzetc.victoria.ac.nz/tm/scholarly/tei-Cyc03Cycl-t1-body1-d6-d12-d2.html>
91. Mr. John Cunningham | NZETC. at <http://nzetc.victoria.ac.nz/tm/scholarly/tei-Cyc03Cycl-t1-body1-d3-d57-d17.html>
92. Obituary. Mrs John Cunningham, Senr. 12 October 1916. *Press* 2 (1916).
93. Resident Magistrate's Court. Albert Bradwell gives evidence. 19 August 1863. *Lyttelton Times* 5 (1863).
94. The Late Fire. Albert Bradwell. 19 March 1870. *Star* 2 3 (1870).
95. Personal Items. Sheddan Brugh Obituary. 2 June 1915. *Hawera & Normanby Star* 4 (1915).
96. Mr William Bush. 23 May 1910. *Press* 7 (1910).
97. News Of The Day. Mr W. Bush. 26 May 1910. *Press* 6 7 (1910).
98. Mr. W. H. Bush | NZETC. at <http://nzetc.victoria.ac.nz/tm/scholarly/tei-Cyc03Cycl-t1-body1-d3-d57-d10.html>
99. Page 3 Advertisements Column 3. Edwin Chappell, Long Bay Road. 13 March 1877. *Akaroa Mail and Banks Peninsula Advertiser* 3 (1877).
100. Akaroa Resident Magistrate's Court. Chappell. 17 October 1882. *Akaroa Mail and Banks Peninsula Advertiser* 2 3 (1882).
101. Farmers | NZETC. William Henry Clement. at <http://nzetc.victoria.ac.nz/tm/scholarly/tei-Cyc03Cycl-t1-body1-d6-d85-d2.html>
102. Obituary. Mrs J. V. Colborne Veel. 17 November 1910. *Press* 6 (1910).
103. Mr. Joseph Veel Colborne-Veel | NZETC. at <http://nzetc.victoria.ac.nz/tm/scholarly/tei-Cyc03Cycl-t1-body1-d3-d57-d70.html>
104. Mary Caroline Colborne-Veel, 1861-1923 - Christchurch City Libraries. at <http://christchurchcitylibraries.com/Literature/People/C/Colborne-Veel-Mary/>
105. Page 1 Advertisements Column 3. William Craythorne, farmer, Lincoln Road. 26 August 1863. *Press* 1 (1863).
106. Resident Magistrate's Court William Craythorne License. 3 May 1865. *Press* 3 (1865).
107. Page 4 Advertisements Column 1. William Craythorne, Rangiora Brewery. 11 April 1872. *Press* 4 (1872).
108. Craythornes Public House. at <http://www.craythornes.co.nz/>

109. Obituary. Mr Thomas Dawson. 22 August 1924. *Akaroa Mail and Banks Peninsula Advertiser* 4 (1924).
110. Old Colonists | NZETC. Day. at <http://nzetc.victoria.ac.nz/tm/scholarly/tei-Cyc03Cycl-t1-body1-d6-d7-d3.html>
111. Obituary. Mr F C. East. 22 August 1916. *Press* 10 (1916).
112. [Prebbleton] | NZETC. Frank East. at <http://nzetc.victoria.ac.nz/tm/scholarly/tei-Cyc03Cycl-t1-body1-d6-d4-d1.html>
113. Obituary. Mrs Adley 24 December 1890. *Star* 4 (1890).
114. News Of The Day. Mr. H. V. Fielder. 11 April 1894. *Press* 4 (1894).
115. Obituary. Henry Fielder. 12 June 1915. *Evening Post* 6 (1915).
116. William Forbes - Information from Relda Smith, descendant. 11 April 2013.
117. Young, Anderson, Forbes, Paterson and connected families - Christchurch - Family History & Genealogy Message Board - Ancestry.com. at <http://boards.ancestry.com/localities.oceania.newzealand.christchurch/99/mb.ashx>
118. Civil Sittings. William Forbes, Bullock driver. 7 March 1860. *Lyttelton Times* 5 (1860).
119. Death. William Forbes aged thirty-eight. 8 March 1877. *Press* 2 (1877).
120. Resident Magistrate's Court. Peter Galletly. 28 January 1869. *Press* 2 (1869).
121. Local & General. Peter Galletly escapes from Sunnyside. 5 January 1884. *Star* 2 (1884).
122. Local & General. Peter Galletly escapes from Sunnyside again. 7 November 1885. *Star* 3 (1885).
123. Biographical Notes Of Settlers Of The First Decade. The Old Identity. 31 March 1898. *Otago Witness* 11 16,12,13,14,15 (1898).
124. Mr. John Grant | NZETC. at <http://nzetc.victoria.ac.nz/tm/scholarly/tei-Cyc04Cycl-t1-body1-d2-d10-d38.html>
125. Obituary. Mr. Jno. Grant. 24 July 1901. *Otago Witness* 19 (1901).
126. Page 2 Advertisements Column 2. Benjamin Hardesty. 22 April 1865. *Lyttelton Times* 2 (1865).
127. Page 4 Advertisements Column 1. Benjamin Hardesty on electoral roll. 5 May 1877. *Press* 4 (1877).
128. Page 8 Advertisements Column 7. Elizabeth Hardesty funeral notice. 20 July 1897. *Press* 8 (1897).
129. Death. Amelia Holmes. 31 October 1885. *Star* 2 (1885).
130. Mr. Carson Henry Horman | NZETC. at <http://nzetc.victoria.ac.nz/tm/scholarly/tei-Cyc04Cycl-t1-body1-d7-d19-d12.html>
131. Turnbull Clan Genealogy Collection A collection of family history submitted by TCA members and friends, currently over 57,000 names. - Person Page 234. at <http://turnbullclan.com/tca_genealogy/tca_all2-o/g0/p234.htm>
132. Old Colonists | NZETC. Mr A. Ivory. at <http://nzetc.victoria.ac.nz/tm/scholarly/tei-Cyc03Cycl-t1-body1-d4-d10-d4.html>
133. Mrs A. Ivory. 19 July 1898. *Star* 3 (1898).
134. Majors of Rangiora, mentions Aquila Ivory. Waimakariri District Council. at <http://www.google.co.nz/url?sa=t&rct=j&q=&esrc=s&source=web&cd=11&ved=0CC0QFjA AOAo&url=http%3A%2F%2Flibraries.waimakariri.govt.nz%2FLibraries%2FLocal_History_-_People%2FMayors_of_Rangiora.sflb.ashx&ei=P6T8UOamEcHFmQW5xoDQDg&usg=AFQj CNECo7PdrQZ0I9IpV9R6Sbb1b1CFjQ>
135. Yaldhurst | NZETC. William Johnston. at <http://nzetc.victoria.ac.nz/tm/scholarly/tei-Cyc03Cycl-t1-body1-d6-d20.html>
136. Obituary. Mrs Abigail McLennan. 13 July 1899. *Star* 1 (1899).
137. Ringwood Estate | NZETC. George MacRae. at <http://nzetc.victoria.ac.nz/tm/scholarly/tei-Cyc03Cycl-t1-body1-d6-d67-d2.html>
138. Obituary. George McRae. 22 June 1911. *Ashburton Guardian* 3 (1911).
139. Old Colonists | NZETC. William James Milner. at <http://nzetc.victoria.ac.nz/tm/scholarly/tei-Cyc03Cycl-t1-body1-d4-d29-d3.html>
140. Obituary. Mrs Milner. 8 April 1910. *Press* 7 (1910).
141. Country News. Mrs Oliver. 29 September 1896. *Star* 1 (1896).
142. Farmers | NZETC. Oliver. at <http://nzetc.victoria.ac.nz/tm/scholarly/tei-Cyc03Cycl-t1-body1-d6-d35-d2.html>
143. Old Colonists | NZETC. Oram. at <http://nzetc.victoria.ac.nz/tm/scholarly/tei-Cyc03Cycl-t1-body1-d4-d1-d4.html>

144. Funeral At Kaiapoi. Mr Charles Oram. 26 November 1900. *Press* 3 (1900).
145. News Of The Day. Henry Paddy. 10 June 1876. *Press* 2 (1876).
146. News Of The Day. Henry Paddy's retirement. 26 August 1882. *Press* 2 (1882).
147. Death. Eliza Paddy. 2 February 1891. *Press* 4 (1891).
148. In Memoriam. Henry Paddy. 2 February 1894. *Star* 2 (1894).
149. Mr Edwin Parnham. 27 July 1911. *Press* 8 (1911).
150. Akaroa. George Scarborough, publican. 26 April 1862. *Press* 6 (1862).
151. Deaths. George Thomas Scarborough. 2 April 1878. *Press* 2 (1878).
152. Page 1 Advertisements Column 4. Funeral notice for George Thomas Scarborough. 2 April 1878. *Press* 1 (1878).
153. Great Grandma's Wicker Basket: James Potts. at <http://greatgrandmaswickerbasket.blogspot.co.nz/2012/07/james-potts.html>
154. Pringle Family history info please. at <http://genforum.genealogy.com/newzealand/messages/7048.html>
155. Deaths. John Pringle, son of John and Agnes Pringle. 12 December 1898. *Otago Daily Times* 2 (1898).
156. Obituary. Mr Ward Robinson. 13 May 1898. *Star* 3 (1898).
157. Obituary. Mr Ward Robinson. 14 May 1898. *Star* 6 (1898).
158. Mr James Rogers. 14 October 1914. *Press* 8 (1914).
159. Resident Magistrate's Court. Walter George Rutland, carpenter, Temuka. 11 April 1878. *Timaru Herald* 4 (1878).
160. Page 3 Advertisements Column 3. Walter George Rutland, bankruptcy, 11 September 1879. *Timaru Herald* 3 (1879).
161. Papers Past — Star — 29 January 1894 — THE NEWSPAPER PRESS. E. R. AKA. Edwin Rutland. at <http://paperspast.natlib.govt.nz/cgi-bin/paperspast?a=d&cl=search&d=TS18940129.2.3>
162. Rutland, E. *[Diary written by the sexton of St John's Church, Invercargill, 1865-1871]* Edwin Rutland. (E. Rutland, 1865).
163. Inquest. Alexander Selfe. 6 January 1866. *Lyttelton Times* 2 (1866).
164. Obituary. Mr Walter Spring. 13 January 1912. *Press* 10 (1912).
165. Disappearance Of Abraham Stubbs. 10 September 1862. *Lyttelton Times* 4 (1862).
166. Resident Magistrate's Court. Suspected Murder of Abraham Stubbs. 8 October 1862. *Lyttelton Times* 9 (1862).
167. Gardening In Canterbury. William Swale, letter to the Editor. 15 March 1866. *Lyttelton Times* 2 (1866).
168. Death. William Swale. 20 February 1875. *Press* 2 (1875).
169. Marriages. William Swale's daughter. 11 October 1878. *Press* 2 (1878).
170. AvonsideParishCemetery.pdf. at <http://christchurchcitylibraries.com/Heritage/Cemeteries/Avonside/AvonsideParishCemetery.pdf>
171. Obituary. Mr. R. D. Thomas. 26 March 1904. *Star* 5 (1904).
172. Page 6 Advertisements Column 6. Henry Wagstaff. Coachbuilder. 22 October 1863. *Lyttelton Times* 6 (1863).
173. Deaths. Mary Ann Wagstaff. 25 March 1887. *Star* 3 (1887).
174. Deaths. William John Ward. 2 January 1899. *Press* 1 (1899).
175. Inquest At St Albans. George H. Wearing mentioned. 14 January 1886. *Star* 4 (1886).
176. Deaths. George Herbert Wearing. 20 June 1893. *Press* 1 (1893).
177. Death. Selina Wearing. 26 January 1911. *Press* 1 (1911).
178. Inquest. Alfred Ambrose Wyatt. 17 August 1895. *Timaru Herald* 4 (1895).
179. Lyttelton. Glentanner passengers. 12 June 1861. *Lyttelton Times* 4 (1861).
180. Shipping Memoranda. Glentanner left same time as Gylfe. 6 July 1861. *Lyttelton Times* 4 5 (1861).
181. Shipping Intelligence. Arrival of the Gylfe. 17 July 1861. *Lyttelton Times* 4 (1861).
182. Shipping Intelligence. Glentanner departs for Callao. 7 August 1861. *Lyttelton Times* 4 (1861).
183. Canterbury. Glentanner arrival and sheep 28 June 1861. *Colonist* 3 (1861).
184. News Of The Day. Mr E. Curry. 16 October 1902. *Press* 4 5 (1902).
185. pringle family info please. at <http://genforum.genealogy.com/scotland/messages/31674.html>
186. Archway :: Item Full Description. Blackford (English Agency) to Provincial Secretary -

passengers per Glentanner. Filed 639 (1) List - 11/08/1857 (R22186389). at <http://www.archway.archives.govt.nz/ViewFullItem.do?code=22186389>

www.ingramcontent.com/pod-product-compliance
Lightning Source LLC
Chambersburg PA
CBHW050655160426
43194CB00010B/1954